T0346721

Evolution of
Economic Ideas

Evolution of Economic Ideas

ADAM SMITH *to*
AMARTYA SEN *and beyond*

Vinay Bharat-Ram

OXFORD
UNIVERSITY PRESS

OXFORD
UNIVERSITY PRESS

Oxford University Press is a department of the University of Oxford.
It furthers the University's objective of excellence in research, scholarship,
and education by publishing worldwide. Oxford is a registered trademark of
Oxford University Press in the UK and in certain other countries.

Published in India by
Oxford University Press
22 Workspace, 2nd Floor, 1/22 Asaf Ali Road, New Delhi 110002, India

First Edition published in 2017
Sixth impression 2022

ISBN-13: 978-0-19-946683-2
ISBN-10: 0-19-946683-1

Typeset in 11/14.5 Goudy Old Style
by Excellent Laser Typesetters, Pitampura, Delhi 110034
Printed in India by Manipal Technologies Limited, Manipal

To
generations of my students at IIT Delhi
and
my family

Contents

Preface   ix

Acknowledgements   xiii

The Great Optimist   3

The Pessimists   12

The Angry Genius   23

The Marginalists   37

The Transition from Political Economy to Economics   42

The Trajectory of Partial Equilibrium Analysis   58

Entrepreneurship and Innovation   74

Money Matters   82

The Saviour of Capitalism   88

The Keynesians   100

The Duel Begins   105

Mont Pèlerin   111

The Great Monetarist   115

The Development Economist   118

The Guru of International Trade   132

Conscience of the Economics Profession   146

Reality versus Theory   163

Bibliography   176

About the Author   183

Preface

When I began teaching economics to business students at the Indian Institute of Technology Delhi more than three decades ago, I realized that the concepts found in most textbooks were received as rather dry and unrelated to the students' day-to-day experience. I tried to bring in a little human touch by relating abstract theories to my own business experience; it helped, but only up to a point. It then struck me that exploring the lives, times, and social circumstances of the various philosophers who gave rise to the ideas that form the foundation of modern economics would be rewarding. I shared these ideas with the class, beginning with Adam Smith, and there was an enthusiastic response.

This book, which takes us on a journey from Adam Smith to Karl Marx, John Maynard Keynes, Amartya Sen, and many others, is a result of those discussions with my students. The chapters explore the subject based on informal interactions with the students. Much of the narrative is inspired by a kind of a Socratic dialogue between teacher and student. Here, I must add that the questions from students are not contrived, but a reflection of the curiosity I encountered over the decades.

The history of economic thought—or the evolution of economic ideas, as I have called it—is not static. If we were to survey some economic historians—Mark Blaug, Bruce Caldwell, Neil De Marchi, Friedrich von Hayek, Frank Knight, Robert Heilbroner, and Mark Skousen, among others—we would find different points of emphasis or interpretation with regard to the same classical thinkers.

Let us take the example of Smith. I quote from *The Worldly Philosophers* (2011), 'He was not in favour of any particular class—specially not the businessman as was the belief in the Thatcher-Regan era.' In fact, as Amartya Sen puts it in his *The Idea of Justice* (2011), 'while some men are born small and some achieve smallness, it is clear enough that Smith has had much smallness thrust upon him'.

The fact is that many in the economics profession even today believe that Smith's focus on achieving prosperity in society is based on man's self-interest. Those familiar with his *The Theory of Moral Sentiments* (1759), however, will appreciate that Smith believed that man was quite capable of empathizing with the suffering of others and playing the role of an impartial observer.

A synthesis of this book would be difficult, if not impossible, since we are talking about thinkers separated by time and space and outlook. Yet a common thread running through all their ideas is that each was a keen observer of the social conditions of his time and was deeply concerned about making a material difference to the economic well-being of the individual and society as a whole. The exciting part is that thinkers commenting on the same social conditions often differed vehemently with one another. To illustrate, if we were to juxtapose Marx with Keynes, both great thinkers, we would see they had a vastly different approach to resolving the ills of humankind. This was reflected in the debates between the Marxists and the Keynesians, especially during the Depression years. Thereafter, during the last three decades of the twentieth century the debate was between the monetarists and the Keynesians, which carried on well into the twenty-first century till the Great Recession of 2008–9. Throughout we see a passion among economists to find the best possible solutions to the human condition, especially when the human condition itself changes over time. Economics, in that sense, is a dynamic pursuit.

This book, I believe, would be of interest not only to students but also to general readers, who could easily skip over the occasional equation if they wish, without losing the thread of the argument.

Acknowledgements

I would like to begin by thanking the late Dev Ranjan Sen who was my colleague for over forty years; then there were professors Amartya Sen, Kaushik Basu, and Dr Nasreen Rehman who encouraged me to take up this project. After I had written the first few chapters, Professor Jagdish Bhagwati perused them and gave me some valuable suggestions. Finally, there was Professor Lord Meghnad Desai who read practically all the chapters and gave me sound advice in tackling certain grey areas where economic historians had diverse opinions. To all of them, I would like to express my heartfelt gratitude, for without their help and encouragement, this book would have been decidedly poorer.

I would be remiss if I did not acknowledge the contribution of Professor N.K. Nair who went through the entire manuscript with a toothcomb looking for editorial errors as well as young Sheikh Mohammed Azharuddin who assisted Professor Nair. Last but not the least, I would like to thank my personal assistant Sangeeta Biswas who typed the entire manuscript.

THE TIME—MORE THAN THREE DECADES AGO

THE SETTING—THE CLASSROOM OF ONE OF
INDIA'S PREMIER INSTITUTES

THE OTHER PARTICIPANTS—YOUNG, BRIGHT MINDS

THE DISCUSSION—ECONOMIC CONCEPTS

THE RESULT—WHAT YOU ARE ABOUT TO READ ...

The Great Optimist

In the mid-eighteenth century, the British, the Dutch, the Portuguese, the Spanish, and the French dominated the seas as well as international trade. What each nation wanted was to accumulate the maximum amount of gold and silver which was known as the system of mercantilism. Each nation would export goods and block imports—the payments for imports being in the form of precious metals. With the underlying belief being that the world's economy is stagnant, its wealth fixed, and that each nation can grow only at the expense of another the governments of these nations authorized monopolies like the East India Company and troops under their command to go forth and colonize the less powerful nations. A natural outcome of this was the confiscation of the gold and silver of the colonized nations.

The seizure of India's treasures has an interesting background. Alexander Dow writes in his *History of Hindostan* (1773) that before the Battle of Plassey in 1757, 'the balance of trade was against all nations and in favor of Bengal'. In fact, he adds, Bengal was 'the sink where gold and silver disappeared without the least prospect of return'. The main exports to Britain and other European countries, despite their high tariffs, were the soft Dhaka muslin and the Indian calico. In the course of the next century, with the British controlling Bengal through the East India Company's private army and through diplomacy, gold—alongside the usual tea and textiles—began making its way out of India and into the British treasury. Adam Smith was horrified at the way 'the company oppresses and domineers in the East Indies', as Nick Robins cites in his *The Corporation that Changed the World* (2006).

Thus while on the one side the mercantilist philosophy dominating British thinking, on the other was the English aristocracy comprising largely of the landed gentry and a smattering of prosperous entrepreneurs and inventors; the Industrial Revolution had yet to gain full momentum. Sylvia Nasar, in *Grand Pursuit: The Story of Economic Genius* (2011), talks about how the powerful upper classes who led lives of elegance and leisure were in dire contrast to the other 90 per cent of the population. The lives of the latter were brutish and short. R.L. Heilbroner, in *The Worldly Philosophers*, talks of the men, women, and children who were lowered into the coal pits of Northumberland and forced to work twelve hours a day. These men, women, and children hardly ever saw daylight in the winter months. Then there were the roving bands of poor peasants looking for work in the countryside.

A student's hand goes up. 'If conditions in Britain in those times were to be compared with India's today, how would we fare?'

It is difficult to compare conditions over such a long span of time. Nevertheless, if an Englishman from that period were to visit today's India, he would most likely be amazed at the prosperity of such a large middle class amidst the poverty of so many.[1]

It was in such a world that Smith was born in 1723 in Kirkcaldy, Scotland. In his youth, he spent six years at Oxford—an experience he regarded as useless—even though he was a good student and read widely on his own. At the age of twenty-eight, he was awarded a chair in Moral Philosophy at the University of Glasgow,

---

[1] For a further discussion on this, see Prasannan Parthasarathi's *Why Europe Grew Rich and Asia Did Not* (2011).

considered a leading centre of learning. Soon enough in 1759 appeared his book *The Theory of Moral Sentiments*, and Smith gained a place among the leading philosophers of the time.

Later Smith was to propound how the self-interest of every man through the influence of 'the invisible hand' brings about social order. However, at this point he still believed that man had the ability to rise above selfishness—to put himself in the position of a third person and thus see the merits of each case as an impartial observer.

In her *Economic Sentiments* (2001), Emma Rothschild, while describing Smith's concept of the 'invisible hand' introduced in his 1759 book, puts it across from a different angle: Smith is describing some particularly unpleasant rich proprietors, who are unconcerned with humanity or justice, but who, in 'their natural selfishness and rapacity', pursue only 'their own vain and insatiable desires'. They do, however, employ thousands of poor workers to produce luxury commodities: 'They are led by an invisible hand to ... without intending it, without knowing it, advance the interest of the society.'

With age, Smith's absent-mindedness became legendary. He would wander in the countryside mumbling to himself. He is said to have once brewed a pot of buttered bread and pronounced it the worst cup of tea he had ever tasted. Another time, while in deep conversation with a friend, he fell into a tar pit.

The students break into laughter. One raises his hand and asks, 'Did Smith ever visit India?'

No, Smith had never been to India, but he went on a most remarkable tour of Europe as a tutor to the young Duke of Buccleuch. There he met Voltaire in France, who had once famously remarked, 'I may disagree with what you have to say, but I shall defend, to the death, your right to say it.' He also met François Quesnay, a court physician and leading French thinker. Quesnay propounded *Le Tableau Économique*, a table for the economy, which in a way foresaw the input–output table for which Wassily Leontief was awarded the Nobel Prize in 1973. Our own five-year plans have used these tables since their inception. However, the problem with Quesnay's table was that he applied it only to agricultural products, insisting that all value creation lay exclusively in agriculture. This, of course, did not make sense to Smith, who believed 'labour could produce wealth wherever it performed, not just on land'.

A young lady raises her hand to ask, 'Did he mean that only labour can produce wealth? What about us who will one day work in offices?'

A good question indeed. However, we must remember that Smith was the first to call Britain 'a nation that is governed by shopkeepers'.[2] Therefore, services were well within his purview, even as he classed them as labour.

It took twelve long years of keen observation of the social scene before Smith's monumental work *The Wealth of Nations* was published in 1776. In it, he argued with great passion and remarkable insight against the prevailing wisdom that wealth depends on the accumulation of gold and silver. Smith revealed how wealth is based on the well-being of the common person. 'No society can surely be flourishing and happy,' he said, 'of which by far the greater part of the numbers are poor and miserable.' He proceeded to explain the laws of the market that give us predictable results in a particular social setting where the drive of self-interest of similarly motivated individuals will lead to competition and how competition will ensure that society gets the goods it desires in the required quantity and at acceptable prices. This will happen because self-interest will guide people towards whatever work the market will pay for. An observation made by Smith in his *The Theory of Moral Sentiments* is quoted often: 'It is not from the benevolence of the butcher, the brewer, or the

---

[2] While it is widely believed that Napoleon was the first to make this observation, it was actually Smith who made this remark in his *The Wealth of Nations*.

baker that we expect our dinner, but from their regard for their self-interest. We address ourselves not to their humanity, but their self-love, and never talk to them of our necessities, but of their advantages.' Further, when self-interested individuals come together as buyers, sellers, and producers, the inevitable result is competition. It prevents profiteering and a glut of unwanted goods in the market, and promotes social harmony.

Many hands go up. 'But this is elementary and we have always known it,' says one student.

This is not quite true. Before Smith, the laws of the market were never expressed with such clarity—how self-interest ensures competition, how prices are kept close to the cost of production, how production is focused only on those goods that are in demand, and how incomes stay in a similar range in diverse lines of production. Considering the times in which Smith lived, it was a tremendous leap into the future. In fact, some believe that Smith anticipated the supply and demand curves and the notion of equilibrium as expounded by William Stanley Jevons, Léon Walras, and Alfred Marshall a hundred years later.

Despite the misery that marked the life of the working person in Britain, Smith observed a rising trend in productivity. He illustrated this using his famous example of the pin factory. It was a small operation employing just ten people where, as Smith observes in his *The Theory of Moral Sentiments*, 'one man draws out the wire, another straightens it, a third cuts it, a fourth points it, a fifth grinds it at the top for receiving the head', and so on. 'Those ten persons, therefore, could make among them upward of forty-eight thousand pins in a day.' Individually, they could 'make twenty, perhaps not one pin in a day....'

The principle underlying this observation was far-reaching. It showed that the division of labour in any factory, big or small, was the secret behind higher productivity. In modern factories to this day, workers operate machines that perform highly specialized functions, and as machines get more sophisticated, the workers' productivity rises. Smith called this the '[u]niversal opulence which extends itself to the lowest ranks of the people'.

'Do you mean Smith could visualize the world we live in today?' a student asks.

Not quite. In today's altered world, we have large monopolistic corporations, powerful labour unions, and governments that are obliged to spend on public welfare as well as levy taxes and duties. Each of them interferes with the price signals that guide consumption and production, as it were, by virtue of a 'hidden hand' in conditions of laissez faire. Yet Smith's system has endured in terms of its broad framework.

From Smith's longer-term perspective, two laws lay behind the market mechanism and the productivity of labour. The first was the law of accumulation, which meant that money saved from high profits must go into machinery, whether in iron foundries or spinning mills, and must thus add to productivity and the division of labour. In those days of early capitalism, profits were generally huge and the urge for investment great. So where did the problem lie? It lay in the accumulation of capital itself, as with greater accumulation the investment in machinery would rise, thus requiring more labour. Gradually, labour would become scarce, wages would rise, in turn squeezing out profits. So what was the solution?

Here Smith's second law comes to the fore. Odd as it may sound, Smith believed—and we quote from his *The Theory of Moral Sentiments*—that 'the demand for men, like that for any other commodity, necessarily regulates the production of men'.

There is a murmur of protest. 'But this is ridiculous,' a student exclaims.

This is what it seems, but consider Smith's reasoning and the state of the society of his time. A greater part of the working man's wages went into feeding himself and his family. Taken in the context of his unstoppable urge to reproduce, it was common for the woman of the house to deliver ten or twenty children with only two surviving. The reason for the high infant mortality was usually malnutrition along with unhygienic living conditions and the frequency of disease. Thus when wages went up, more children survived and over time the labour force swelled. The accumulation of capital became profitable as wages declined in consequence of a greater competition for jobs. This cycle went on, with profits rising and falling in response to the supply and demand for labour.

In Smith's view, just as prices regulated the consumption and production of goods, wages over the long run regulated profits. In a way, it was a logical self-correcting construct of society. As innovation and induction of better machines resulted in accumulation, society in Smith's view would grow wealthier in perpetuity. Was this true? Yes, to the extent that Britain's per capita income went up from USD 1,000 in Smith's time to just over USD 4,000 by 1900 and to USD 18,000 by the end of the century, as mentioned by Skousen in his *The Making of Modern Economics* (2001).[3]

Yet Smith could not have foreseen the advent of the Industrial Revolution, the pressure of population on land, the gradual overwhelming of the landed aristocracy by the capitalist class, and the conflict between labour and capital.

Smith's enduring contribution stands out nevertheless. He was not in favour of any particular class—especially not the businessperson as was the popular belief in the Thatcher–Reagan era. As cited in *The Worldly Philosophers*—and often quoted elsewhere—according to Smith, '[P]eople of the same trade seldom meet together even for merriment and diversion but the conversation ends in a conspiracy against the public, or in some contrivance to raise prices.' His views on the role of government were also clear. He believed in minimal government interference in the market mechanism and was strongly opposed to trade barriers. This is evident from a telling comment by him cited in Skousen's *The Making of Modern Economics*: '[W]hat is prudence in the conduct of every private family, can scarce be folly in that of a great Kingdom ...If a foreign

---

[3] The figures mentioned here are in terms of the 1995 USD rate.

country can supply us with a commodity cheaper than we ourselves can make it, better buy it of them....'

Another observation made by Smith has great relevance in
contemporary times. Prior to the advent of industrialization, there
was greater equality in the level of consumption than when productivity increased and the aggregate level of consumption went
up. While the rich gained hugely compared to the workers, the
workers' level of consumption was considerably higher than it
was in earlier times, say in feudal societies. According to Smith,
this would continue to be the case as productivity and prosperity increased. Thus, there is a dilemma here, which Marx dwelt
upon at length a century later. Would we wish to be poorer and
equal to the other members of society, or would we prefer to be
richer among poorer members of society, given a greater disparity
of incomes? This dilemma continues to plague the modern world
by driving a wedge between, say, those in favour of globalization
and the anti-globalizers, between the small percentage of the very
rich and the wage and salaried classes.[4]

It is hard to summarize the contribution of Smith who was not
only an economist but also a sociologist, historian, and philosopher. His The Wealth of Nations marks a turning point in the way
the Western world looked at economic problems. Nevertheless,
it is important to take note of a perceptive observation made by
Amartya Sen in his The Idea of Justice: '[W]hile some men are born
small and some achieve smallness, it is clear enough that Smith
has had much smallness thrust upon him.' This has reference to
the fact that many in Smith's own lifetime and many in the economics profession today believe that Smith's primary focus in the
achievement of prosperity in society was on man's self-interest or
selfishness. The truth was—especially those who have read his The
Theory of Moral Sentiments would appreciate this—that Smith's view

[4] For a detailed discussion on this, see Thomas Piketty's Capital in the
Twenty-First Century (2013).

of man was quite well-rounded. Smith believed that man was quite capable of empathizing with the suffering of others as well as taking upon himself the role of an impartial observer. Indeed, Smith provided a holistic edifice, which has held together in essential ways despite attacks from future generations of economists and rapidly changing times.

Smith died in 1790 at the age of sixty-seven, a long span considering the times. Towards the end of his lifetime, he received all the honours and accolades he richly deserved. Only his alma mater ignored him.

The Pessimists

The civil servants who peopled the East India Company were trained at its college in Haileybury, which was established especially for this purpose. Thomas Robert Malthus, the son of an eccentric intellectual, held the first chair in political economy. Born into a higher-middle-class family in 1766 and educated at Cambridge in mathematics and languages, he went on to become a cleric for the Church of England in 1788. He ceased being a cleric when he married in 1794 but was later known as reverend until his death in 1834. A disciple of Smith, Malthus, along with his friend and associate David Ricardo, was destined to alter Smith's wonderful world view.

It is important to understand the general mood in Europe and England at the turn of the eighteenth century. It was one of optimism, with a profusion of Utopians and romantics like Nicolas de Condorcet and Richard M. Goodwin who were regarded as men of the Enlightenment, and science triumphed over superstition and faith. They also believed that the growth of population was good for the progress of humankind. Laissez faire was the dominant economic philosophy in France. Thinkers like Jean-Baptiste Say and Frédéric Bastiat not only supported Smith's ideas on free enterprise and free trade but also built upon them.

To this day, Say is famous for propounding what is known as Say's Law. According to this law, supply creates its own demand. This implies that there can never be a glut in the market because when goods are sold, the price they fetch goes into the pockets of those who produced them in the form of wages, rent, profit, and interest. That entire sum comes back to the market for the purchase of the next round of goods and services—this includes some for the purchase of consumer goods and the rest for that of capital goods.

'So what's wrong with that argument?' a student asks.

Say did not give weightage to the fact that consumers could save instead of spending. One-hundred-and-thirty later, Keynes showed the importance of saving and spending in the economy. In the intervening period, Malthus provided some insights into this problem. Among Say's many accomplishments, one of the most noteworthy is his defining of the term 'entrepreneur' as one who brings together capital, knowledge, and labour to manage a business for profit.

But let us move back to Malthus, who published his highly controversial *An Essay on the Principle of Population* in 1798. The book was actually his argument against Goodwin's and Condorcet's views on the benefits of population growth. It goes to show how little we understood about the population problem that post-Independence India's first prime minister Jawaharlal Nehru is believed to have remarked that for every extra mouth to feed we will have two extra hands to work. This is also a part of the reason why the population problem was not taken seriously for decades after Independence.

As Skousen mentions in his *The Making of Modern Economics*, Malthus's basic thesis was that 'the power of population is indefinitely greater than the power of the earth to produce subsistence for man'. In other words, while there is a tendency for population to increase geometrically (1, 2, 4, 8, 16...), food production tends to increase arithmetically (1, 2, 3, 4, 5...). These 'laws of nature' that Malthus called 'incontrovertible truths' had enormous implications. They reinforced Smith's cyclical movement in the demand and supply of labour with greater emphasis. This is to say that with growing population, food shortages would become more acute, causing greater numbers in the working classes to die, thus bringing wages back to subsistence levels. No wonder this was called the *iron law* of wages.

Malthus's further observation—that charity would actually increase suffering since it would lead to more breeding of children and put further pressure on the food supply—was scandalous to Christian values. He also opposed the British welfare system that provided relief to the poor and the unemployed based on the size of the family. Malthus regarded this as rewarding the idle—those who would feel encouraged to marry early and proliferate at the cost of the taxpayer. As Nasar notes in *Grand Pursuit*, Malthus's argument was so persuasive that parliament passed 'a new poor Law in 1834 that effectively restricted public relief to those who agreed to become inmates of Parish poor houses'.

No wonder Charles Dickens, a keen observer of the social scene from the drawing rooms of the rich to the plight of the poor, wrote so touchingly about life in a Parish poor house in *Oliver Twist* (1838). He described life in a factory town called 'Coke Town' with its foul air and workers as slaves to their machines with equal poignancy in his *Hard Times* (1854). Dickens, however, was a positive thinker who believed that man could overcome all adversity (as he himself had) and after his visit to the United States, he was doubly convinced that with millions of acres of untilled land waiting to be cultivated, there could be no shortage of food for man.

'But Dickens was no economist; he was a novelist,' says a student.

Indeed, Dickens was no economist, but men of literature, poetry, and the arts sometimes have a feel for things that practical people often fail to see. His remark that 'political economy is a mere skeleton unless it has a little human covering, and filling out, a little humanity bloom upon it, and a little human warmth in it', published in his weekly *Household Words*, is particularly tell-ing. Malthus though, however unpopular his views were in his time, had made a correct assessment of the mismatch between the means of sustenance and the urge to reproduce.

Let us see how Malthus's prognosis has held up in the more than 170 years since his time. In India, the green revolution cer-tainly warded off a dire situation and we have had a surplus of foodgrains ever since. Sub-Saharan Africa continues to be on the margins of subsistence but America, as Dickens had predicted, has become a huge food surplus country feeding different regions of the world in times of need. As Skousen observed in his *The Making of Modern Economics*, animals and poultry reproduce much faster than humans do and thus provide alternative sources of food. This, of course, ignores the fact that animal feed takes up much more land than humans would require for an equivalent quantity of foodgrain consumption.

Then there is the other side of the problem—the population growth rate. The Western countries, Russia, Japan, and Australia have long achieved replacement or less than replacement levels, that is, zero or negative population growth. China, likewise, has halted its growth rate with its controversial one-child policy. India was a cause of concern for long but in the last two decades, the population growth rate has been falling with Kerala attaining zero growth and the south, north, and west coming quite close to that milestone. The east is still a cause of concern despite its falling growth rate. Yet let us not forget that the world's popula-tion in Malthus's time was just 1 billion and 170 years later it stands in excess of 7 billion. We may ignore his warning at our own peril.

In the later editions of his essay on population, Malthus clari-fied that on account of 'the great barrenness of a very large part of the surface of the earth—and by the decreasing proportion of produce which must necessarily be obtained from the continual addition of capital applied to land already in cultivation', food output will tend to decline. The world today knows this very important principle as the law of diminishing returns.

Another rather fumbling but important observation contradicting Say's Law was that depressions or 'general gluts' were possible, without of course elaborating that saving may exceed spending. This observation, though refuted by the logical and more articulate Ricardo, was to become a central concern of Keynesian economics a century later.

Ricardo, a friend and contemporary of Malthus, was a pessimist for a different set of reasons. He was born in 1772 into a Jewish family. After spending two years at a Hebrew school in Amsterdam, he joined his father at the London Stock Exchange. However, he became a Unitarian after marrying a Quaker at the age of twenty-one and his father disinherited him. Ricardo went on to amass a huge fortune over the years as a stockjobber and government-loan contractor and became the richest economist in history.

Unlike the somewhat underrated Malthus who contributed in no small measure to Thomas Carlyle's labelling economics a dismal science, Ricardo was much admired in his own lifetime and influenced the subsequent generations of economists.

Among the most famous of his many contributions—something that is used to this day by trade economists—is his law of comparative advantage. It is perhaps best to state it in his own words.

To quote from 'On Foreign Trade' that appeared in *The Principles of Political Economy and Taxation* (1817):

The quantity of wine which [Portugal] shall give in exchange for the cloth of England is not determined by the respective quantities of labour devoted to the production of each, as it would be if both commodities were manufactured in England, or both in Portugal.

England may be so circumstanced that to produce the cloth she may require the labour of 100 men for one year, and if she attempted to make the wine, it might require the labour of 120 men for the same time. England would therefore find it in her interest to import wine and to purchase it by the exportation of cloth. To produce the wine in Portugal might require only the labour of 80 men for one year, and to produce the cloth in the same country might require the labour of 90 men for the same time. It would therefore be advantageous for her to export wine in exchange for cloth. This exchange might even take place notwithstanding that the commodity imported by Portugal could be produced there with less labour than in England. Though she could make the cloth with the labour of 90 men, she would import it from a country where it required the labour of 100 men to produce it, because it would be advantageous to her to rather employ her capital in the production of wine, for which she would obtain more cloth from England than she could produce by diverting a portion of her capital from the cultivation of wines to the manufacture of cloth. Thus, England would give the produce of the labour of 100 men for the produce of the labour of 80.

If we were to put this down in the form of a chart, it would appear as follows:

Number of workers per unit	England	Portugal
One unit of wine	120	80
One unit of cloth	100	90

In case no trade takes place between the two countries, each would have one unit of wine and one of cloth. However, if the two countries contemplated trade, it is clear that Portugal would have an absolute advantage in the manufacture of both products. Nevertheless, if Portugal were to get all its workers to make wine, it would have 170 workers making 2.125 units of wine. Likewise, if England were to get all its 220 workers to make cloth, it would have 2.2 units of cloth. This means that in the event of trade there would be 20 per cent more cloth and 12.5 per cent more wine available. Each nation should therefore specialize in those products in which it has a comparative advantage.

This was indeed a remarkable and brilliant discovery which at first glance appears counterintuitive. A free-trade theorist like

Jagdish Bhagwati would swear by it in his earlier writings, arguing that it would bring about greater prosperity for the world as a whole. See, for instance, Bhagwati's 'The Pure Theory of International Trade: A Survey' that appeared in the *Economic Journal* in 1964. In retrospect, it is true that since Ricardo's time, import duties in the US have indeed come down from 50 per cent to less than 5 per cent.

Nevertheless, this idea faced opposition from many countries, especially from the developing nations who believe that the human dislocation of labour in existing trades is not always worth the cost. This is evident from the protests that we witness at the venue of the international conferences related to the General Agreement on Tariffs and Trade (GATT) in different parts of the world.

When in 1847 the Bank of England suspended the gold standard as a result of the cost of war, Ricardo argued vigorously for it to be reinstated. He explained in his major study *The High Price of Bullion* (1811) how an excess of bank notes issued by the Bank of England was the prime cause of inflation. This is why some people attribute the quantity theory of money to Ricardo.

A student asks me to explain, to which I respond by requesting patience, as I shall come back to it when we discuss Irving Fisher in the 1930s.

Ricardo is credited alongside Malthus for discovering the law of diminishing returns. Only the way he developed it led to major implications.

As the demand for corn (wheat and barley) rises, according to Ricardo's argument, less fertile lands would be called into use, which would result in a declining yield per acre. Further, since land was constant for a country, the increasing use of less fertile land requiring higher inputs like labour and implements would raise the cost and, consequently, the price of corn. Two things would happen. The wages of labourers would have to rise to enable them to subsist and those who owned the more fertile lands would benefit from the difference in the cost of production of corn being incurred by them and by those with less fertile lands. Ricardo called this differential *rent* or a benefit for which the landlord puts in no effort. The rise in wages, on the other hand, while keeping labour at a subsistence level would squeeze out profit over time so that in the end the only beneficiary would be the landlord. Rent was therefore a form of unearned income, which would finally result in a conflict between the landlord, the entrepreneur, and labour.

'Why was Ricardo considered a pessimist?' asked a student.

Ricardo was considered a pessimist because he believed that the marginal output of corn would diminish over time as less and less fertile land was brought into use. Taken together with Malthus's theory of population growing at a geometric rate, the outlook was indeed bleak. Despite Ricardo being a strong advocate of free trade and arguing vigorously for the repeal of the corn laws that protected the interest of the landlords through high tariffs on imported corn, he understood that the lobby of the landlords in parliament was too deeply entrenched to permit such a repeal. It was only in 1846, more than two decades after Ricardo's death in 1823 at a young age of fifty-one, that the corn laws were repealed. One of the positive consequences of England being flooded with cheap corn thereafter was that it became the workshop of the world. For the next seventy years or so, British industry dominated practically every nation.

Ricardo never foresaw this during his own lifetime. Instead, he believed, as reflected in a letter he wrote to Malthus, cited in Skousen's *The Making of Modern Economics*, that '[p]olitical economy, you think is an enquiry into the nature and causes of wealth [Smith's view]; I think it should rather be called an enquiry into the laws which determine the division of the produce of industry among the classes who concur into its formulation.' He supported his contention by arguing that with the increasing use of less fertile land, rents to the owners of fertile land would rise and as wages rise, profits would fall. As he puts it in the same letter, 'In proportion then as wages rose, would profits fall.' Rising wages, however, would induce workers to have more children, thus augmenting the supply of labour with the result that 'the iron law of wages' would ensure a tragic outlook for workers. In consequence, landlords, entrepreneurs, and workers would forever be in opposition—an idea later picked up by Marx.

Ricardo's obsession always was to discover an 'invariable measure of value'. Unlike Smith who believed that market forces played a key role in the determination of price, Ricardo focused on the quantity of labour units, not wages, as the true measure of value. Although he was aware that items like old wines and rare paintings have little connection with labour units, he regarded these as exceptions to the general rule. Machinery, too, he regarded as nothing but accumulated labour. Here was another powerful idea picked up by Marx.

However, before we turn to Marx, we need to take note of John Stuart Mill, a leading political economist in the tradition of Ricardo and the son of the famous historian James Stuart Mill. The life of John Stuart Mill (1806–1873) spanned a fascinating period in the British history. It was a time when intellectuals, horrified by the harshness of capitalism spawned by the Industrial Revolution, turned towards a Utopian form of socialism. The famous names associated with this form of socialism included, among others, Robert Owen of New Lanark, the industrialist who demonstrated the benefits of humane approach to capitalism; Jeremy Bentham who propagated the pleasure-pain principle in economics that could be likened to modern cost-benefit analysis; and, of course, Beatrice and Sidney Webb who towards the end of the century ushered in Fabian socialism, which in later years greatly influenced India's Nehru.

As their icon, the Utopian socialists chose John Stuart Mill, the greatest political economist of their time. Mill never went to school or college, and was homeschooled by his father. As a result, he read Greek when he was three, and had read Aristotle and Plato among many others by the time he was eight. By the age of eleven, Mill was proficient in calculus and geometry and had read Newton's *Principia Mathematica*. Further, having absorbed all the classical economists, he carried forward the influence of Ricardo and the utilitarianism of Bentham.

Most in the class are agape. A student asks, 'How was that possible?'

I honestly did not know. All I could add was that by the age of twenty, Mill had a nervous breakdown from which he, of course, recovered. One could get a glimpse into his character from a statement he once made to a friend: 'I was never a boy.' Despite brief relapses into depression, especially after his father's death, Mill found happiness in the company of Harriet Taylor, whom he married after she was widowed.

As regards Mill's core contribution to economics, it is best to express it in his own words. In his *Principles of Political Economy* (1848), he says, 'The laws and conditions of the production of Wealth partake of the character of physical truths. There is nothing optional or arbitrary in them.' Distribution is an entirely different story. Mill adds: 'It is not so with the Distribution of Wealth. That is a matter of human institution solely. The things once there, mankind, individually or collectively, can do with them as they like. They can place them at the disposal of whomsoever they please, and on whatever terms. The distribution of Wealth depends on the laws and customs of society.'

In *The Making of Modern Economics*, Skousen mentions how Hayek had, not surprisingly, remarked: 'I am personally convinced that the reason which led the intellectuals to socialism ... was John Stuart Mill.' In summary then, Mill dissociated the laws of distribution from those of production. This is to say that once wealth is produced, it is for society to distribute it according to its laws and customs. As Skousen cites in *The Making of Modern Economics*, Mill, in his essay 'Of the Influence of Consumption on Production', called it a 'pernicious doctrine' and a 'palpable absurdity'.

A hand goes up. 'But this doesn't make sense.'

'You will never make a good socialist,' I said jokingly, 'though you will soon see how powerful Mill's ideas turned out to be.'

On the issue of rent, Mill agreed wholeheartedly with Ricardo to the extent that when he worked for the East India Company, he argued strongly for the nationalization of land in India. This, in fact, followed from Ricardo's idea that landlords were mere rent earners and did no productive work.

Mill's 'personal philosophy', as Skousen puts it, 'was Laissez Faire: Individuals are free to act as long as they do no harm to others'. His classic work *On Liberty*, first published in 1859, bears testimony to this.

The Angry Genius

A spectre is haunting Europe–the spectre of Communism. All the Powers of old Europe have entered into a holy alliance to exorcize this spectre: Pope and Czar, Metternich and Guizot, French Radicals and German police spies.... The Communists disdain to conceal their views and aims. They openly declare that their ends can be attained only by the forcible overthrow of all existing social conditions. Let the ruling classes tremble at a Communistic revolution. The proletarians have nothing to lose but their chains. They have a world to win. Working Men Of All Countries, Unite!

In 1848, these words were written as part of *The Communist Manifesto*[1] by Karl Marx and his compatriot Friedrich Engels. Skousen cites this in *The Making of Modern Economics*.

It is indeed a coincidence that a spectre was haunting Europe at the time. A revolutionary fervour in the air cut across Paris, Belgium, Berlin, Italy, Prague, and Vienna. So fragile did the old order seem that for a time Louis Philippe of France abdicated the throne only to come back later. The Belgian monarch actually submitted his

---

[1] All those interested in Marx or Marxism should read *The Communist Manifesto*, a pamphlet in actuality, by accessing it on the Internet and thereby experience the stirring words that have over the years converted countless young men and women around the world to Marxism.

resignation. Mobs of industrial workers and motley crowds rioted in Paris, Italy, Prague, Vienna, and Germany, with Paris as the epicentre of this revolution.

John Kenneth Galbraith describes an event in the revolution in his colourful language in *The Essential Galbraith* (2001):

The workers succeeded in getting to the Place de la Bastille and in building a formidable barricade. The first attack by the National Guard was repelled, and some thirty guardsmen were killed. The romantic tendencies of revolutionaries now asserted themselves. Two handsome prostitutes climbed to the top of the barricade, raised their skirts and asked what Frenchman, however reactionary, would fire on the naked belly of a woman. Frenchmen rose to the challenge with a lethal volley.

Despair among the workers was reflected in the songs they sang in their foundries and workshops. However, there was no coordinated programme of action and after much bloodshed things returned to the way they were.

For Marx and Engels this was not a matter of disappointment. Their programme was aimed for the long term and in Marx's words, it was a part of the 'inexorable' march of history. It was based on the following tenets:

1. Expropriation of property in land and application of all rents of land to public purposes
2. A heavy progressive tax
3. Abolition of all right of inheritance
4. Confiscation of the property of all emigrants and rebels
5. Centralization of credit in the hands of the state, by means of a national bank with state capital and an exclusive monopoly
6. Centralization of transport in the hands of the state
7. Extension of factories and instruments of production owned by the state; the bringing into cultivation of wastelands, and

the improvement of the soil generally in accordance with a common plan

8. Equal liability of all to work. Establishment of industrial armies, especially for agriculture
9. Combination of agriculture with industry, promotion of the gradual elimination of the contradictions between town and countryside
10. Free education for all children in public schools. Abolition of children's factory labour in its present form. Combination of education with industrial production, and so on

Who was Marx and what did he really stand for? Let's take a journey back in time to Germany's oldest town, Trier. It was here that Marx was born in 1818 to a Jewish family. His entire life bears testimony to his being a man of contradictions: he was raised in a bourgeois family, but he despised the bourgeoisie; he was born a Jew—his father later converted to Christianity—yet he perceived them as beings for whom money was their worldly God; his writings focused on improving the condition of the industrial worker, but there is no proof of him ever visiting a factory.

Marx chose to live in poverty for fifteen years of his life even though he belonged to an upper-middle-class family. Despite his love for his children, he saw them die of malnutrition or suicide; of his six offsprings, only two survived him. A Prussian police spy, Saul K. Padover, who visited Marx in his apartment in Soho in London described him in *Karl Marx: An Intimate Biography* (1978) as:

Marx is of medium height, 34 years old; despite his relative youth, his hair is already turning gray; his figure is powerful.... His large, piercing fiery eyes have something uncannily demonic about them. At first glance one sees in him a man of genius and energy.... In private life he is highly disorganized, cynical person, a poor host; he leads a real gypsy existence. Washing, grooming, and changing underwear are rarities with him; he gets drunk readily. Often he loafs all day long, but if he has work to do, he works day and night ... very often he stays up all night ...

Two girls put their finger and thumb to their nose. 'Be serious,' I said. There is more to Marx, much more.

When Marx was attending the University of Bonn, his father found out that he was spending his time in drinking and indulging in rowdy behaviour. He had Marx transferred to the prestigious University of Berlin, where he spent five years and came under the influence of the German philosopher Georg Wilhelm Friedrich Hegel. It was from Hegel that Marx absorbed the concept of 'dialectics', which was to become the backbone of his future research. On completing his PhD thesis in Greek philosophy amidst great fear of rejection as anti-Hegelians had taken over the university administration, Marx submitted it at the University of Jena, where it was accepted.

In 1843, Marx married Jenny von Westphalen, the daughter of a wealthy German aristocrat. Marx had known Jenny since his child-hood. Soon after their wedding, they moved to Paris. In the new city, Marx became the editor of a German monthly magazine. It was in Paris that he first met Engels. Engels was two years younger and went on to become Marx's shadow as well as his source of financial assistance for the rest of his life.

The two men, both German, could not have been more different. Marx was swarthy of complexion, powerfully built and of medium height, and had 'jet black hair that sprouted from his cheeks, arms, nose and ears'. He was boorish albeit immensely well-read in literature, poetry, philosophy, history, science, and political economy. It was said that Marx was generally busy arguing in cafes or wading through oceans of books, going without sleep for days on end. His English was ponderous and he spoke with a heavy Teutonic accent, but so convinced was he of his own viewpoint that he was utterly intolerant of another.

It was Heilbroner who had used that adjective to describe Marx in his *The Worldly Philosophers*. 'I am going to annihilate you'—this was how Marx would often open his conversations, as one of his associates later recalled, a reflection of how Heilbroner's reading of Marx was right.

Marx was soon expelled from Paris for propagating revolution in Germany. He then moved to Brussels where he was jailed for arming Belgian workers with rifles purchased from his own inheritance. Eventually, in 1849, he moved to London where he spent the rest of his life.

On the other hand, Marx's colleague Engels was considered tall and of a military bearing, even though he stood just at five feet and six inches. Engels was the son of a prosperous industrialist who owned textile mills in Germany and Manchester. He was posted in Manchester where he made a success of running the family business in spite of his abhorrence of it. His heart really lay in observing the condition of the working classes around him. To that end, he wrote *The Condition of the Working Class in England* in 1844, a work that influenced Marx greatly, especially in focusing his attention on political economy.

Hegel, too, had a profound impact on Marx during his years at Berlin University. It was from Hegel that Marx picked up the idea that '[c]ontradiction is the root of all motion in life' as cited by Skousen in *The Big Three in Economics* (2007). In other words, the dialectic between two opposing forces will bring about a new force. Every thesis has the seeds of its own antithesis within it, which results in a synthesis and in turn becomes the new thesis.

As Skousen elucidates in his *The Making of Modern Economics*, Marx drew upon the example of how in the early times slavery was the key mode of production. Then, according to Hegel–Marx dialectic, with the coming of the middle ages feudalism became its antithesis and thereafter during the Enlightenment a synthesis emerged in the form of capitalism. The antithesis of capitalism would be socialism, which would inevitably lead to communism.

The detailed arguments behind this process are contained in Marx's classic work *Das Kapital* or *Capital*. Its first volume was published in 1867, by when he had already prepared notes on volumes II and III. However, as they remained in draft form till his death in 1883, they were published posthumously by Engels. The popular version of Marx's ideas is based on Volume I, which he updated for later editions. This will be the subject of discussion hereafter.

A student wants to know more about the two volumes published later.

In a historical perspective, Marx was convinced that socialism would sound the death knell of capitalism. The question was by what logic. Axiomatically, Marx drew upon Ricardo's labour theory of value, which later Mill endorsed. According to this theory, the value of a 'commodity' is based on the number of labour hours that go into its making and, most importantly, labour is the sole producer of value.

'But how can that be?' a student wonders aloud. I ask the students to simply stick with Marx's reasoning for a while.

Marx proposed a theory of 'surplus value', which comprised profits and interest. Since surplus value was created solely by labour, it followed that capitalists and landlords were the exploiters of labour.

According to Marx's mathematical formula,

$$p = s/r$$

where p is the rate of profit,

s is surplus value or exploitation, and

r is the value of the final product.

According to conventional wisdom, the value of the final product should be its sale price. However, Marx defined it as two forms of capital, namely constant capital c and variable capital v,

where c takes the form of the plant and equipment and v is the
cost of labour. The extended formula would then be:

$$p = s/v+c$$

Marx contended that the relation between labour cost and
the labour hours expended would not remain constant since
machinery and technological improvements would benefit the
capitalist and not the worker. Further, since the hours worked
could be extended and women and children employed at lower
wages, exploitation would only rise with additional investment in
capital equipment.

Marx countered the argument that capital required a reasonable return by saying that capital was nothing but 'frozen' labour.
The entire value of the final product should thus go to labour in
the form of wages. Furthermore, with the rise in the investment
in capital, the exploitation of labour would also rise. The classical economists offered no rebuttal, but a few years later Eugen
von Böhm-Bawerk of the Austrian School argued that capitalists
deserved a fair return for entrepreneurship and risk-taking.

In *The Communist Manifesto*, Marx had observed that '[t]he
bourgeoisie, during its rule of scarce one hundred years, has created more massive and more colossal productive forces than have
all preceding generations together'.

Capitalists, therefore, are prone to accumulating more and
more capital in the form of machinery and newer technology.
However, based on the formula

$$p = s/v+c,$$

this will mean that as c increases, s will decline and the rate of
profit p will be driven down. Such concentration of capital will
further imply that in pursuance of economies of scale, large firms
will absorb or drive out small businesses. The big fish will devour
the small, thus causing more unemployment and misery, which
will eventually lead to the creation of an 'industrial reserve army'.

Marx further observed in *The Communist Manifesto* that capitalists are engaged in the relentless 'conquest of new markets, and by the more thorough exploitation of the old ones'.

Marx, in fact, looked upon the East India Company's invasion of Indian territory as a positive development, as he felt it would hasten the decline of feudalism and bring about the rise of capitalism in India, which in terms of his theory of 'dialectic materialism' was part of the inexorable march of history. Marx, in other words, would have suggested waiting till feudalism was destroyed and capitalism was established before the exploitation of the industrial worker began as a prelude to socialism.

This observation by Marx has been interpreted by many Marxists, including those in India, to mean that imperialism is the same as globalization, even though the former, as understood in the pre-Second World War era, came to a close especially after most colonies gained their independence in the two decades that followed the war. Indian Marxists to this day, nevertheless, believe that foreign direct investment, especially from America, is a trojan horse that is the thin edge of imperialistic designs.

At the end of Chapter 32 of Volume I of *Capital*, Marx explains in his inimitable prose how the development of capitalism actually takes shape:

As soon as this process of transformation has sufficiently decomposed the old society from top to bottom, as soon as the labourers are turned into proletarians, their means of labour into capital, as soon as the capitalist mode of production stands on its own feet, then the further socialization of labour and further transformation of the land and other means of production into socially exploited and, therefore, common means of production, as well as the further expropriation of private properties, takes a new form.

That which is now to be expropriated is no longer the labourer working for himself, but the capitalist exploiting many labourers. Thus expropriation is accomplished by the action of the immanent laws of capitalist production itself, by the centralization of capital. One capitalist always kills many.

Hand in hand with this centralization, or this expropriation of many capitalists by few, develop, on an ever extending scale, the co-operative form of the labour-process, the conscious technical application of science, the methodical cultivation of the soil, the transformation of the instruments of labour into instruments of labour only usable in common, the economizing of all means of production by their use as the means of production of combined, socialized labour, the entanglement of all peoples in the net of the world market, and with this the international character of the capitalistic regime....

The Capitalist mode of appropriation, the result of the capitalist mode of production, produces capitalist private property. This is the first negation of individual private property, as founded on the labour of the proprietor. But capitalist production begets, with the inexorability of a law of Nature, its own negation. It is the negation of negation. This does not re-establish private property for the producer, but gives him individual property based on the acquisitions of the capitalist era: i.e., on co-operation and the possession in common of the land and of the means of production.

The transformation of scattered private property, arising from individual labour, into capitalist private property is, naturally, a process incomparably more protracted, violent and difficult than the transformation of capitalistic private property, already practically resting on socialized production, into socialized property. In the former case, we had the expropriation of the mass of the people by a few usurpers, in the latter, we have the expropriation of a few usurpers by the mass of the people.

This passage shows the millenarian vision of Marx. Four ideas emerge from it. First, as the old feudal society transforms itself, the labourers who till their own land and artisans who work with their own implements 'are turned into proletarians' by the newly emerging capitalist who groups them together to suit the capitalist mode of production. Their labour is thus transformed into capital, furthering the process of exploitation. Second, 'one capitalist always kills many'. What this means is that capitalism's inherent tendency towards greater centralization to gain economies of scale eliminates not only small businesses but leads to greater socialization of labour (which is not too different from Smith's division of labour). This culminates in their exploitation or expropriation. Third, through 'the entanglement of all peoples in the net of the world market', capitalism takes on a global character. Finally, as the despair and misery of the workers grow, they unite as a disciplined 'industrial army' to overthrow their tormentor, the capitalist.

Marx moreover believed that the growth of capitalism is not a steady process. He explained this idea in *The Communist Manifesto*: 'It is enough to mention the commercial crises that by their periodical return put on its trial, each time more threatening, the existence of the entire bourgeois society.'

Thus, economic depressions are inherent in the capitalist process and each time they occur, they not only cause greater unemployment but also threaten the very existence of the capitalist system. This brings us to the imminence of the collapse of the capitalist system.

The moot question was how soon would this collapse occur. While writing Volume I of *Capital*, Marx worried that the capitalist system might collapse before he completed the work. By the time he got to volumes II and III, his tone was more mellow and his style more analytical. The inevitability of the collapse of the system was not denied, but he never specified or predicted how soon it would happen. This has been a subject of vigorous debate between Marxists. Meghnad Desai delineates a different take on it in his *Marx's Revenge: The Resurgence of Capitalism and the Death of Statist Socialism* (2002). According to Desai:

It has been taken for granted, even by some high authorities, that in *Capital*, Marx provided an analytical argument for the breakdown of capitalism.... Yet what we discover is that on reading *Capital*, one could conclude that capitalism will live through cycles, and a slow as well as cyclical tendency of the rate of profit to decline. As capitalism grows, it spreads globally, and its crises become worldwide. But could it be that Marx provides a better argument for the long-term survival of capitalism than his detractors or followers have given him credit for?

Another dilemma faced by Marx was the 'transformation problem'. Some industries are capital-intensive and others are labour-intensive. Since Marx argues in the first volume of *Capital* that prices vary directly with labour time, it follows that capital-intensive industries will be less profitable than labour-intensive ones. However, there is evidence to show that over time profitability in all industries tends to be nearly the same as capital migrates from the less profitable to the more profitable ones. Marx struggled with it throughout his life, but he could never resolve this 'transformation problem'.

'What you have said so far sounds like a very interesting story, but what about the contradictions in his reasoning?'

A good point, indeed. We shall see later how the great Austrian economist Böhm-Bawerk addressed the issue.

In the meantime, let us examine Marx's description of the evolutionary role of money, a concept he explained in the third chapter of *Capital*, and what has come to be regarded as an important contribution even by those with a capitalist bent of mind.

There are four stages to this process. It begins with a simple barter between commodities such as three shirts for a pair of trousers or five goats for a cow. This is expressed as:

$$C - C'$$

Thereafter, when money enters the transaction, it is shown as

$$C - M - C'$$

Here money is simply a means to facilitate the exchange between two commodities. Such an exchange takes place not only between the consumer and the producer, but also when a manufacturer buys components and sub-assemblies that go into the final product. Marx, however, felt that there is a very thin line between 'making money' and 'making useful goods and services'. This he shows as follows:

$$M - C - M'$$

Here money M is used to produce C, which is sold for M'. M' represents more money than the price inclusive of normal profit. One could think of speculation on a scarce commodity or being part of a cartel to charge monopoly prices, or being party to 'crony' capitalism where businesspersons collude with politicians in power to make supernormal profits.

'Is this not what we see happening in India today?' This is simply not a common question, but more of a common concern that the students seem to have.

Crony capitalism is definitely for real. Certain politicians and businesspersons make more money in a few years than honest businesspersons could make over two or three generations.

Here money becomes the primary motive rather than the production of goods and services, which is—and should remain—the main object of economic activity. The focus thus shifts from C to M.

The next step is the final one, where commodities do not feature at all in the exchange process:

$$M - M'$$

Think of equity markets or bond markets on the stock exchanges, or options and derivatives and new financial products. Try to connect them with the production and consumption of real goods and services. You will find that there is hardly a connection between them. According to Marx, this is the stage of mature capitalism, and it will herald its downfall. Marx's prediction came to a dangerously close realization during the Great Recession different story to which we shall return later.

Finally, how do we evaluate the contribution of Marx? During Marx's own lifetime, the real wages of workers rose steadily despite some recessionary dips. In fact, the fifty years prior to 1914 could be regarded as a period of unprecedented prosperity in the Western world. It was also a period of near complete globalization, as there were hardly any trade barriers. Thus, interestingly, none of Marx's predictions were fulfilled during his lifetime.

In such a setting, *Capital* sold barely a thousand copies. Marx might have died in relative obscurity but for the fact that Engels had *Capital* translated into Russian in 1872. This was to fall in the hands of one Vladimir Ilyich Ulyanov or Lenin, which sparked his interest in Marxism and the rest, as they say, is history. Leopold Schwarzschild, in *The Red Prussian: The Life and Legend of Karl Marx* (1947), famously iterated that without Marx there would be no Lenin and without Lenin, no Marx. Galbraith also pays Marx a memorable tribute in *The Age of Uncertainty* (1977), where he says, 'Not since the prophet has a man's influence been so little diminished by his death.'

The story of Lenin's steady rise is long enough to easily fill a book. It suffices to say that he studied Marx in depth—at Marx's desk at the London Museum where Marx devoted years to research and writing—and later applied his own interpretation to *Capital* to eventually transform Tzarist Russia into a communist state. The fact that communism interpreted by Lenin and later reinterpreted by Stalin lasted a full seventy years after the end of the First World War is an indirect tribute to Marx. The tribute is indirect owing to the fact that Marx never visualized the transformation of a society as feudal and monarchical and, most importantly, as nascent in the development of capitalism as Russia to be the first to establish a socialist-communist state. In line with his concept of 'dialectical materialism', Marx believed that the first to experience the collapse of capitalism and the advent of socialism would be the industrialized nations like Britain, France, and Germany where their 'industrial reserve army' of workers would be ranged against the capitalist system. This did not happen largely because some of the demands in *The Communist Manifesto*, barring the expropriation of private property, such as gradual—not heavy—progressive taxation, the centralization of public transport, abolition of child labour in factories, and so on were implemented over time. Moreover, the steady rise in the standard of living of workmen and the eventual recognition of the right of collective bargaining took the steam out of any revolutionary fervour.

'*But what about its success in Russia?*' *a student asks.*

Lenin's role in the conversion of Russia into a socialist–communist state began with the October Revolution of 1918—a full thirty-five years after Marx's death.[2]

[2] For a simple account of Lenin's success and failure, see Galbraith's *The Age of Uncertainty*.

The Marginalists

There was a time when further progress in political economy was moribund. In his *Principles of Political Economy* (1848), Mill wrote, 'Happily, there is nothing in the laws of value which remains for the present or any future writer to clear up; the theory of the subject is complete.' Marx, too, had borrowed heavily from Ricardo, even though he had given his own interpretation to the future of capitalism. As Heilbroner writes in his *Marxism: For and Against* (1980), Marx's ideas on political economy may have proved to be flawed, but Marxism survives.

It was only in the early 1870s that three thinkers from different countries came up with more or less the same path-breaking idea. They were Carl Menger from Austria, Jevons from Britain, and Walras from France. Jevons and Walras, in fact, compared their breakthrough to the discovery of calculus.

As Skousen mentions in his *The Making of Modern Economics*, many attribute the 'neoclassical' revolution in economics to the Austrian School. This school marks the starting point of our discussion here. Menger (1840–1921) is believed to have first introduced the concept of marginal utility, which was translated into English much later. Hayek (whom we shall meet in a subsequent chapter) referred to Menger as 'a man of extraordinarily impressive appearance' in his *Choice in Currency* (1976).

The beautiful city of Vienna, with its university at which Menger taught, its museums, palaces, opera houses, and cafes on the banks of the Danube river was indeed a place that attracted intellectuals, artists, and musicians from all over Europe in the mid-nineteenth century. Apart from a generation of great economists, there were musicians like Mozart, Beethoven, and Brahms, and of course the great resident psychologist Sigmund Freud. Many decades later, the well-known Indian psychologist Sudhir Kakar and music conductor Zubin Mehta would be trained there.

Menger argued in his famous work *Grundsätze* (1871), which was translated later as *Principles of Economics* (1890), that the value of a good was determined not by labour inputs, as Ricardo and Marx believed, but by the satisfaction of the consumer who paid for it. Value thus depended on the consumer rather than the producer, a contradiction of what Ricardo and Marx had proposed. The price of a good, moreover, followed from its next best use, a concept close to the marginality principle. If the demand for a particular good falls, its price will decline and so would the prices of the labour and capital involved in its production to their next best use.

'Isn't this like opportunity cost?' a student asks.

It is. Menger was also of the view that economic progress depended not so much on the division of labour as 'on the gradual and constant increase in the range of goods and service, and the improvement in their quality', as quoted in *The Making of Modern Economics*.

In a final blow to the classical school, Menger argued that there is no such thing as the 'intrinsic value' of a good; that it depends on supply and demand. As we shall soon see, he was not the only one to discover this.

In a brief digression from marginal economics, let us talk about Menger's most illustrious disciple Böhm-Bawerk (1851–1914) who was one of the stalwarts of the Austrian School and to whom we had referred in the chapter on Marx. Marx, it will be recalled, believed that all surplus value as defined by him belonged to labour, and that profit and interest were nothing but a measure of the exploitation of the working man. Böhm-Bawerk countered this notion by arguing that while the worker is paid regularly, say monthly or weekly, the capitalist has to wait until the final product is sold and the cash recovered. The waiting time could be short or it could be much longer in case of recession. Profit and interest, in that sense, are compensation for 'waiting' and what the worker gets is a discounted value of the future sale. Furthermore, the capitalist could go bankrupt and lose everything unlike the worker who would be paid at regular intervals. There was thus always an element of 'risk' undertaken by the capitalist, for which he deserved to be compensated. These arguments form the core of Böhm-Bawerk's *Karl Marx and the Close of His System* published in 1898. Böhm-Bawerk thus demolished a central premise of Marxian economics.

On the other hand, like the classical economists, Böhm-Bawerk, too, laid great stress on the role of thrift and saving as the key to investment and growth. That he de-emphasized the role of consumption was to become a point of controversy well into the twentieth century.

Returning to the marginal revolution, let us discuss the life and ideas of Jevons (1835–1882). England after Marx and Engel's *The Communist Manifesto* was on a growth track with the Industrial Revolution forging ahead. By 1870, it was indeed a prosperous nation. Jevons contributed significantly to economics in his short life, even though he had studied chemistry and biology at University College, London. Mathematics was his forte, which he applied to his own understanding of political economy after having read the classical economists, especially Ricardo and Mill. Jevons scoffed at the idea that value is based on the cost of production as well as the notion of a 'natural rate of wages'. Like Menger, with whom he was not familiar, he believed that 'value depends entirely upon utility', as quoted in *The Making of Modern Economics*.

'Isn't it a bit one-sided?' asks a student.

A good point, indeed. Jevons, in fact, made an acute observation, quite correctly, that a consumer will spend on different products to the extent where their marginal utilities are equally proportionate to their price. In other words, for products x, y, z:

$$\frac{Mu_x}{P_x} = \frac{Mu_y}{P_y} = \frac{Mu_z}{P_z}$$

This idea was elaborated in Jevons's *Theory of Political Economy* (1871), which, though regarded as brilliant, did not go far enough in propounding the demand and supply functions. That work was left to the great Cambridge economist Marshall.

While the new ideas of Menger and Jevons that prompted the marginalist revolution began with their respective publications in 1871, those of Léon Walras (1834–1910) who went much further were published in their complete form only in 1874 under the title of *Elements of Pure Economics*. Walras is famous not only for contributing to the marginal revolution but also for inventing the general equilibrium theory. What this theory says is that given free competition, price flexibility, and mobility of factors of production, it is possible to put together a series of simultaneous equations for the whole economy, such that the number of equations is equal to the number of unknowns. It follows that the free market system will necessarily lead to a general equilibrium, with the supply and demand for all goods in the economy being equal—a mathematical proof in a sense of Smith's central ideas. For years, indeed well into the twentieth century, Walras's ideas were sidelined as too intricate or at best an explanation for a static economy. This was not altogether true, for he did develop an auctioneering model by which it was possible to shuffle or grope towards the equilibrium position.

'Why aren't we taught this? It sounds brilliant.'

It is brilliant but is generally believed to be too abstract and somewhat far removed from the real world.

As for the marginal revolution, we will analyse its eventual completion and broader implications in the following chapter.

The Transition from Political Economy to Economics

Alfred Marshall (1842–1924) is credited with advancing classical economics—political economy—into a quantitative science. This was how 'economics' was born. In 1890, the first edition of Marshall's *Principles of Economics* was published, which redefined the way the subject is taught today.

When I studied economics in the mid-1950s at Delhi University's St. Stephen's College, *Principles of Economics* served as our textbook. With other well-known textbooks like Samuelson's *Economics: An Introductory Analysis* (1992 [1948]) not readily available to us, we heavily relied on Marshall's text. Over the years, some of Marshall's concepts have stayed with me even as they have been refined and elaborated further. Marshall, the son of a bank cashier and the grandson of a butcher from his mother's side, was born in the East End of London in a noxious tannery district. However, he was not proud of his family antecedents and preferred not to speak about them.

The 1860s was a time when only about one in a hundred could break out of a lower status in society and climb up the social ladder to the middle class—it was almost like a lower-caste person in India aspiring to attain a higher caste status. Middle-class status in England, of course, was defined by a liberal or non-vocational education, an upper-class accent, and a reasonable income level. All of these were necessary to qualify as a gentleman.

Marshall was a bright student and had a special talent for mathematics.[1] At the age of seventeen, much against his father's wishes who wanted him to study the classics and join the church, Marshall chose to pursue his dream to study mathematics instead. He took a loan from an uncle in Australia and with a scholarship at St. John's College, Cambridge, enrolled to pursue his dream of studying mathematics. Marshall also successfully completed another challenge at the end of three years as he earned his Mathematical Tripos with a high score that guaranteed him a comfortable income and a lifetime fellowship at his college. The question arises: did his meteoric rise make Marshall forget those less fortunate than himself?

On the contrary, Marshall got deeply interested in the condition of the 'working man' who became his 'patron saint'. Marshall's interest shifted gradually from mathematics to the betterment of humankind and to this end he applied his mastery of statistics and observation of facts at the micro-level. Nasar cites Marshall's aim in *Grand Pursuit* as follows: 'the desire to put mankind into the saddle is the mainspring of most economic study.'

Unlike his predecessors Ricardo, Mill, and Marx who had never actually visited factories or seen the condition of the working class first-hand, Marshall took a deep interest in observing the workman in his workplace as well as his living conditions, making detailed notes in his 'red book'.

[1] Nasar has written an endearing account of Marshall's youth and his travels in America in Chapter 2 of *Grand Pursuit*.

A real breakthrough in Marshall's view of social change was realized when he visited the United States of America in 1875. The civil war was over, slavery had been abolished, the transcontinental railway had recently been completed, and the union had held together. Marshall travelled from Niagara to San Francisco, part of the journey on the new railroad, then on a paddle boat down the Mississippi, and from Cheyenne to Denver on a twenty-four-hour stagecoach ride, before heading to San Francisco.

'Do you think Marshall might have come across cowboys and bandits as we see in the movies?'

I am not sure about the bandits, but Marshall did come across new settlements in the making and he must have seen cattle drives and cowboys. In fact, what he saw was a new civilization unfolding before his eyes.

Marshall's most acute observations were about a uniform access to a decent education, a certain 'go' and optimism in the eyes of people, and a propensity on the part of workmen to better their material condition by improving their productivity on the job, or moving to an alternate profession. This was quite unlike the apprenticeship system in Britain, which tied the workman to his job due to the lack of a proper education and a fatalistic attitude going back in time to the iron law of wages. Nevertheless, Marshall held a strong belief that educating workers could boost productivity and, consequently, lead to a rise in wages. He, in partnership with his wife Mary, devoted a great amount of his time for this purpose.[2] Marshall married Mary Paley, an extraordinary and intellectually gifted woman, after his return from the US. When Marshall encouraged Mary to complete her Tripos in political economy, she willingly took up the challenge and became one of the first women to be awarded a degree at the University of Cambridge.

[2] Small and steady improvements in productivity were formalized a hundred years later by the Japanese under the 'Kaizen system', something that is much in use in the modern industry.

Alfred and Mary made a handsome couple and while Mary devoted her time to educating women, Alfred remained busy collating his experiences for his magnum opus *Principles of Economics*.

The controversy about whether production (supply) or utility (demand) is the determinant of value had been continuing for decades. Marshall came up with a simple proposition, uniting the two schools of thought, by suggesting that like two blades of a pair of scissors, both supply and demand are necessary in the determination of value. Just as one cannot attribute the cutting of paper to the upper or the lower blade, value cannot be attributed to either demand or supply.

'But is this so profound an idea?'

Some of the most obvious ideas take generations to unfold— whether in the sciences or the arts.

Indeed, Marshall gave the world its first economics textbook. The book elucidates how markets behave, how firms plan their production, and how factors like land, labour, capital, and management come together. Moreover, it talks about different industries as aggregates of firms in the same business and their behaviour over time.

Marshall illustrated many of his arguments in his book using diagrams. The most seminal of these is where he draws the demand and supply curves to show the point of equilibrium along with the explanation.

Marshall also cautioned that this equilibrium will hold on the assumption that the prices of substitutes and competing products from within the country or abroad remain frozen. Furthermore, as the figure refers to a single market and a single product rather than the whole economy, it shows a position of partial equilibrium. It is also implicit in Marshall's reasoning that the demand curve based on the law of diminishing marginal utility tends to slope downwards whereas the supply curve that is shown as sloping upwards follows the law of diminishing returns on production. However,

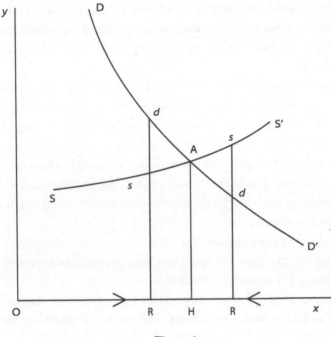

Figure 1

Source: Marshall (1952 [1920]: 200).

under certain conditions the supply curve could be horizontal or downward sloping but at a slower rate than the demand curve so that both intersect at a certain point.

The demand curve shown by Marshall is, in effect, Jevons's diminishing marginal utility curve for each consumer against the price he is willing to pay for each additional unit of a good summed up for all the consumers of that good in the market. Indeed, the demand curve can also be referred to as the average revenue curve.

The supply curve represents the output of all the firms in the industry offered for sale at different prices. The point at which the supply curve intersects the demand curve is known as the point of equilibrium. A shift to the left from this point shows that the supplier firms are not taking full advantage of the demand curve, which then indicates that the consumers are willing to buy more quantity at prices higher than the supply price. A move to the right of the equilibrium point shows that consumers are not willing to pay the supply price. Hence, at the equilibrium point the supplier firms make the maximum profit and the consumers derive the maximum possible satisfaction.

A student raises his hand and asks, 'Where has Marshall used marginal analysis that the earlier philosophers discovered?'

This can be shown through diagrams or mathematically. I ask the students for the preferred mode.

'Through mathematics,' the class spoke in unison.

I was not surprised. They were, after all, students of engineering.

It is important to remember that marginal means the price the consumer is just willing to pay for the next unit of consumption, or, as Jevons would say, where the marginal utility just equals the price. On the supply side, marginal means the cost of production of an additional unit of production. For arriving at the optimal level of production and sale, we can follow the steps shown below:

Profit (π) = Revenue (R) – Cost (C) for quantity (Q)

Since π is maximum at the point of equilibrium,

$$\frac{\partial \pi}{\partial Q} = 0$$

$$\frac{\partial (R - C)}{\partial Q} = 0$$

$$\frac{\partial R}{\partial Q} - \frac{\partial C}{\partial Q} = 0$$

$$\frac{\partial R}{\partial Q} = \frac{\partial C}{\partial Q}$$

or Marginal Revenue = Marginal Cost.

R and C are both functions of Q and we now know the optimal amount to be produced and sold. This will be true whether the supply curve is horizontal or downward sloping, as Marshall indicates in the figure. It will also be true for a firm or industry.

An example of a horizontal supply curve can be shown in the case of bottled drinking water. There are many supplier firms in Delhi that sell at a price of around Rs 20 a bottle. The demand of each customer is limited, but for all customers in the market the demand curve could be downward sloping or even horizontal. Why horizontal? Because if the bottlers raise their price even a little, customers will shift to tap water and home purifiers. This means that the demand is infinitely elastic—a discussion we will return to later.

Assuming that the capacity for purifying and bottling water of the supplier firms is practically unlimited, the industry supply curve will be horizontal. We can thus have an equilibrium when the demand curve is horizontal only if the supply curve slopes upward.

The case of a downward-sloping supply curve is quite interesting, as it implies that the supply price of a product declines over time through, what Marshall calls, external economies—a rather common occurrence in the electronics industry. A cell phone available in the market today may be priced slightly higher than the one bought a year ago, as the newer model would be equipped with newer features, or the year-old phone today could be much cheaper than it was at the time of purchase. In other words, the price performance ratio would be to the advantage of the producer and the consumer—the reason being that steady investment in research and development brings about a steady decline in the cost of inputs like computer chips, as a result of which the whole industry benefits. Those benefits in turn are shared between the producers and consumers. On the other hand, external diseconomies could also force the supply curve upwards, instances of which are evident in industries that pollute the environment, like chemicals and steel. These industries may have to invest heavily in pollution-control equipment, which would raise costs and hence the cost curve.

Two of the most useful concepts that Marshall invented by applying mathematics to economics were *elasticity* and *consumer's surplus* and these have been much used in welfare economics. We have talked about the different slopes of the demand curve, but not about their implication, which is captured by the concept of elasticity of demand:

$$e = \frac{\%\Delta Q}{\%\Delta P}$$

Here, e is the elasticity and Q is the change in the quantity of a product bought in response to a change in the price of that product. This helps in answering questions of great practical importance to firms. As in the case of bottled water, a small increase in price by one firm could cause loss of market share to competitors, or a general increase by the whole industry could trigger a switch to tap water purified at home.

The demand, however, will be deemed inelastic (the demand curve tending to vertical) where a change in price will have a minimal impact on the quantity sold. This can happen if there is a monopoly of some essential product or service, as in the case of a single manufacturer of a lifesaving drug or a monopoly of health services.

The elasticity concept has been applied to taxation policies all over the world. Finance ministers at the time of formulation of the budget have to worry about the amount of revenue created by estimating whether a certain percentage increase in a tax would raise the revenue or decrease it. This can be done by estimating the tax elasticity. To find out the level of impact of a reduction in income tax on demand, they can estimate the income elasticity. Governments have commonly raised taxes on cigarettes to discourage smoking.

Now we move on to Marshall's other major contribution—his concept of consumer's surplus. There is normally a single price in the market at which buyers buy and sellers sell their product. However, according to Jevons's notion of declining marginal utility, some of the buyers willing to pay a certain price for a commodity would be pleasantly surprised to find that they actually have to pay less. They would thus enjoy a consumer's surplus of satisfaction. This is a common experience with those who go to a mall expecting to buy a pair of shoes or a handbag at a certain price but find the product being offered at a discounted price, with them having to pay less than what they expected. The following diagram shows how Marshall presents this concept:

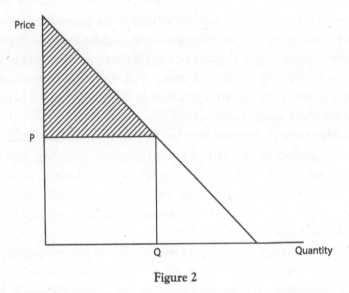

Figure 2

Source: Author.

The shaded area shows the consumer's surplus when the market price of, say, mangoes is P. This is so because the customers who are willing to pay a higher price than P derive added satisfaction.

❧❧

Two other concepts that need to be clarified are: one, the cost structure of the firm; and two, Marshall's concept of the short, medium, and long term. The costs a firm incurs can be divided into fixed costs, which do not vary at all as output changes, and variable costs, which change with changes in the output. The total costs are a summation of these two types of costs.

Accordingly, a firm has to invest in fixed assets like machines and buildings as well as management before beginning production. Once production commences, it makes use of labour, raw materials, power, and so on, the requirement for which increases as output increases. Here it is important to understand the difference between variable cost and marginal cost. Variable cost begins at an output level of zero, whereas marginal cost begins at the level of constant fixed cost. Since the latter is the cost of an additional unit of production, it reflects the change in the total cost for that one extra unit. The point of equilibrium where marginal cost equals marginal revenue has already been discussed.

Marshall's concept of time, another extremely important contribution, has been briefly explained by Samuelson and William Nordhaus in *Economics* (1992) as:

At the turn of the century Cambridge University's great Economist Alfred Marshall helped forge the supply-and-demand tools we use today. He noticed that demand shifts produce greater price adjustments in the short run than in the long run. We can understand this observation by distinguishing three time periods for market equilibrium that correspond to different cost categories: (a) momentary equilibrium, when supply is fixed, (b) short-run equilibrium when firms can increase their output even though plant and equipment are fixed, and (c) long-run equilibrium, when all factors are variable, so firms can abandon old plants or build new ones and new firms can enter or exit the industry.

It follows that if there is a sudden increase in demand in the industry, firms will first exhaust their stocks and, in the process, the supply curve will move towards a vertical position. As the firms add more capacity, the supply curve will tend to flatten, and finally if demand prevails in the whole industry, it can tend towards infinity. It should be further noted that in the long run all costs are variable since plant and machinery can also be added or treated as sunk costs.

Marshall is often referred to as 'the father of microeconomics'—distinct from macroeconomics, which we shall discuss later. While thousands of textbooks have been written based on Marshall's work, we present here only some points of departure.[3]

It is important to note the contribution of two of Marshall's intellectual heirs, namely Joan Robinson (1903–1983) from the University of Cambridge, UK, and Edward Chamberlin (1899–1967) from Harvard University, US. It was one of those rare coincidences of history that both these economists came out with more or less equivalent theories in 1933—the Theory of Imperfect Competition by Robinson and the Theory of Monopolistic Competition by Chamberlin. While Robinson moved on to write about a range of other topics in economics, Chamberlin spent much of his life arguing about how monopolistic competition was different from imperfect competition.

'Were the two theories really different?' a student asks.

When I studied at St. Stephen's College, *The Economics of Imperfect Competition* (1954) was used as a textbook, while in the US students studied *The Theory of Monopolistic Competition* (1933). Both the books are essentially the same except for the message the two authors have tried to convey. Samuelson has commented on this issue in his *On the History of Economic Analysis: Selected Essays* (1967): 'Indeed the time has come when we may permit ourselves to use the terms monopolistic competition and imperfect competition interchangeably, emancipating them from their first associations with the different conceptions of Chamberlin and Mrs. Robinson, using them as convenient names for the best current models of price theory.'

We shall discuss the differences between monopolistic competition and imperfect competition later. Marshall's central idea, it is important to note, brought the classical and marginalist schools

---

[3] For a more exhaustive understanding of microeconomics, Samuelson and Nordhaus's book *Economics* (fourteenth edition) is strongly recommended.

together in his supply and demand diagram. He also had a clear
concept of the industry as comprising of firms engaged in producing an identical product, the demand for which was sensitive only
to price. Furthermore, if each firm accounted for a tiny percentage of the industry, it could sell any amount of its product at the
market price. That is, it would face a horizontal demand curve—a
situation of perfect competition and the free entry and exit of
firms in the industry.

A real-life example of this can be observed in the cotton spinning industry in India. There are nearly 2,000 spinning mills in
India catering to the weaving business. Each spinning mill, however large, is a small part of the whole industry—thus more or less
fulfilling the conditions of perfect competition. In the event that
high consumer demand coincides with a good cotton crop, the
whole industry benefits; if this condition sustains over a period
of time, new firms tend to enter the market. However, if demand
declines and cotton prices are high—possibly because of a poor
crop—firms other than the most efficient ones begin to face losses.
This can be diagrammatically represented as follows:

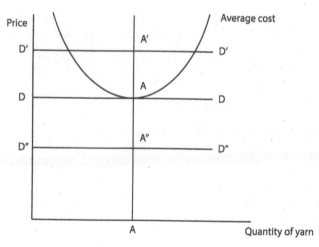

Figure 3

Source: Author.

Note that the average cost curve of the typical firm is tangential to the demand curve DD at quantity A. This shows that at that point the firm is making normal profit, which under competitive conditions is just enough to sustain it. Were the market conditions to improve, it would then make extra-normal profit equal to DAA'D'; if the condition prevails, more firms will enter the industry. Conversely, in adverse circumstances with lower demand, the typical firm would make losses equivalent to DAA"D".

But what is the average cost curve? We can explain this with the figure below:

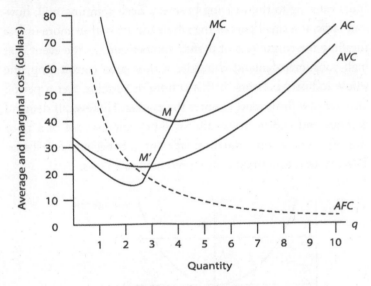

Figure 4 Cost Curves

Source: Samuelson and Nordhaus (1992 [1948]: 123).

Note: All cost curves can be derived from the total cost curve: a) the total cost is made up of fixed cost and variable cost, and b) the curve of marginal cost falls and then rises. $AC = TC/q$, $AVC = VC/q$, and $AFC = FC/q$. Also, $AC = AVC + AFC$. Note that MC intersects AC at its minimum.

At this stage, a horizontal demand curve has purposely not been shown because Robinson and Chamberlin posit a departure from Marshall. Marshall believed that in the long run firms would face a perfectly competitive situation, and that a downward-sloping demand curve would be a short-run phenomenon. This is because the firms are free to enter or exit an industry, and as an industry typically comprises a large number of firms, a perfectly competitive position would be restored in time. This, in fact, would be compatible with Smith's laissez faire argument along with maximizing social welfare.

Robinson and Chamberlin argued that perfect competition was an exception rather than a rule, and that in the long run firms would face a downward-sloping demand curve. The reason for this being that first, an industry does not necessarily comprise of many firms, and second, with economies of scale that follow from high fixed costs, there are barriers to entry and exit.

'Entry is obvious, but why exit?' a student asks.

The reason for it is that firms can survive and tide over bad times so long as their revenues cover average variable cost, and if there is a good chance that the market will revive to a point where they will make normal or extra-normal profit, the firms will stay on.

With regard to a downward-sloping demand curve, note that firms can exercise some market control; of course, not as much as a monopolist who faces a vertical demand curve, but somewhere in between that and a horizontal one, or an elasticity of demand between zero and infinity. In other words, if the firms are not in collusion, which is against the law in most free market economies, and are competitive, they can gain some market control through product differentiation, advantages of location, and advertising. In today's markets, say, branded shoes that have the same utility value as a regular pair command a much higher price on account of the brand image. The same is the case with cars, where manufacturers spend enormous amounts on advertising and develop a kind of customer loyalty. To illustrate, say, a Toyota car and a Honda car are in the same price bracket and Toyota raises its price by a small amount. This move may not affect Toyota's market share. If, however, the price rise is high, then some customers may shift to Honda, but not all customers still would. This is because Toyota has created a significant brand loyalty. This again illustrates another Marshallian principle of cross-elasticity of demand between close substitutes, that is, if A raises its price, then B will gain market share, and vice versa. At the other end, even salt is being branded and sold as a differentiated product. In fact, the entire marketing profession is largely based on product differentiation. Consequently, perfect competition is getting confined to a narrow band of commodity markets.

'So how does a firm reach equilibrium?'

In the long run, equilibrium under monopolistic (or imperfect) competition is as shown below:

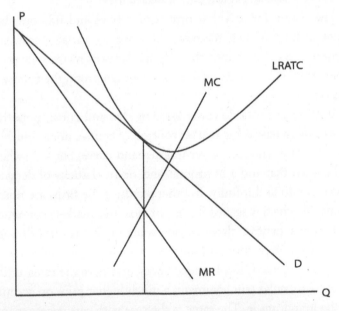

Figure 5 Long-run Equilibrium in Monopolistic Competition

Source: Bellante (2004).

One can observe that the demand curve is tangential to the long-run average total cost curve, but it is so at a point prior to that of minimum cost, which lies where MC intersects LRATC. This means that equilibrium and minimum cost do not synchronize as they do under perfect competition. It follows that there is surplus capacity, which taken in aggregate for all firms is socially undesirable.

Robinson acknowledged this but more in the context of labour, which she felt would be exploited since, presumably, if capacity were not fully utilized, it would lead to less than the potential employment of labour. In any event, she saw a departure from perfect competition as evidence of market failure, which means that the free market was not able to ensure equilibrium at lowest cost and, in consequence, was not conducive to maximum welfare. Hence, state intervention was needed.

Chamberlin, on the other hand, believed that monopolistic competition was a reality and a sign of vigorous competition whereby product differentiation and innovation went hand in hand. Although he did not push this point, it undoubtedly echoes the great Austrian economist Joseph Schumpeter whose work will be discussed later in this book.

To conclude this discussion, we can establish that Marshall marked the transition from classical to neoclassical economics, which used mathematics for partial equilibrium analysis for the first time, and changed the trajectory of economics in a direction that continues to influence a large part of the economics profession.

The Trajectory of Partial Equilibrium Analysis

In 1933, forty-three years after the publication of Marshall's *Principles*, Robinson and Chamberlin came out with their own theories. This was a period during the interwar years when countries of the free world had become more inward-looking and consequently world trade declined perceptibly. Not surprisingly, the microeconomics of the time focused on national economies without paying much attention to the outside world. It was surprising though that this focus continued into the postcolonial world when international trade was on a growth path, not just because of the post-war prosperity of the Western nations but also due to the rapid growth of the Asian economies. Microeconomics textbooks to this day, nevertheless, confine themselves to closed economies.

'What exactly is partial equilibrium analysis?' a student wants to know.

I realized that I should have explained that earlier. Partial equilibrium analysis examines the conditions for equilibrium of a product in a market assuming that the prices of all other related products and factors of production are given. In other words, the product in question is insulated from any feedback effects of changes in the prices of related products or factors of production. Such feedback effects can only be examined under general equilibrium analysis.

꧁꧂

Moving on, however, in the post-war period—1966 to be precise— Indira Gandhi's government announced a devaluation of the Indian rupee vis-à-vis the US dollar by 36 per cent. This event would not have had any immediate impact for DCM Limited, the company where I worked, but for the fact that it had signed up for the import of a USD five-million plant to manufacture rayon tyre cord, part of which was on the high seas. This meant that if the whole plant was imported, the cost would go up by 36 per cent, which would have had a significant impact on the economics of the project. However, the dispatch of a bulk order of spinning machines was pending. We cancelled the import of these machines and instead obtained a few sample machines that were then copied by our engineers at a fraction of the import price. Thus the total project cost was kept in check.

This is a case of how an exchange rate depreciation gave an impetus to import substitution (the replacement of imported items by indigenous items), which was achieved by a combination of ingenuity and drive by our engineers.

In the broad spectrum, a number of public and private sector companies in India went in for creative import substitution in the decade that followed.[1] However, as a downside of this, import substitution in India, like in some Latin American countries, was driven by policy rather than sound economics. India aimed at 'self-reliance' and 'freedom from foreign dominance' as specified by the Planning Commission of 1969. The result was a rather autarchic approach to import substitution, which gave it a bad

[1] For a detailed analysis, see Bharat-Ram's *Towards a Theory of Import Substitution Exchange Rates and Economic Development* (1982).

name. It must be remembered that prior to the reforms of 1991–2 initiated by Manmohan Singh, the then finance minister in the Narasimha Rao government, India was a closed economy. It was subject to foreign exchange controls wherein imports for industry were approved on a case-by-case basis, and keeping the rupee value way above its open market price ensured that imports would be cheap while exports would remain unviable. As a result, the country faced severe balance-of-payments constraints, which came to a head in 1991.

In contrast, Japan followed a policy of creative import substitution in the post-war years. Many works have covered this with reference to the development of Japan's automobile industry. Kaname Akamatsu's 'A Theory of Unbalanced Growth in the World Economy' (1961), Kiyoshi Kojima's *Japanese Direct Investment Abroad* (1989), and Ippei Yamazawa's paper titled 'Full Utilisation of Foreign Trade and Industrialisation: East Asian Experiences' (1958) are significant works in this context. They talk about how the British Austin, the French Renault, and the American Willys were closely examined by the leading Japanese auto manufacturers and copied. Each component was examined for its local manufacturability.[2] Eventually, a vehicle with some domestically manufactured and some imported parts emerged for the local market. Later, with greater experience and progressively higher levels of import substitution, economies of scale lowered the cost structure, making the product more viable in the export market. With time, further improvements and modifications were introduced. This pattern was repeated in a wide range of industries, transforming over time the macroeconomic structure of Japan as a whole.

A number of other East Asian countries, namely the Republic of Korea, Hong Kong (now part of China), Taiwan, Singapore, Indonesia, Malaysia, and Thailand followed Japan's example and registered incredibly high growth rates from the 1950s onwards.

[2] See also Cusumano's *The Japanese Automobile Industry* (1989).

Not surprisingly, the *World Bank Policy Research Report* (1993) named these countries as the 'East Asian Miracle' economies. Despite differences in detail regarding their economic policies, these countries had some common features. They recognized the need for rapid growth in a changing world economy and placed the right emphasis on fundamentals, such as high levels of domestic savings, the development of broadly based human capital, minimal price distortions, an accent on exports, and sound macroeconomic management. This also meant a control on budget deficits and inflation, and the monitoring of exchange rates and external debt. China in the 1980s under Deng Xiaoping and India in the 1990s under Narasimha Rao followed suit, thus transforming their respective national economies.

'Is this about the developing economies only?' a student wants to know.

In my opinion, despite a general impression that import substitution is applicable only to the developing or emerging economies, it is equally relevant for the industrially advanced economies.

Let us consider the example of Japan in the 1980s. By this time, Japan had built a huge trade surplus and flooded the world markets, particularly the US, with consumer products like cars, televisions, watches, cameras, and so forth. In consequence, the value of Yen skyrocketed, thereby making it difficult for Japan to export its manufactures, particularly its cars, which were growing in popularity in the US. Japan reacted by setting up assembly plants in the US for its popular models of Toyota, Nissan, and others. With the local production of some of the components in the US with Japanese technology and American labour, the cost witnessed a considerable reduction. It was thus a win-win situation for both countries.

In the case of China, which pegged its currency to the US dollar at an artificially low rate, the outcome was different. China flooded the world markets, particularly the US, with cheap goods, and eventually built a formidable pool of foreign exchange reserves. The US, Japan, and other developed countries found it difficult to break into the Chinese home market with fully built-up products. So, as in the case of cars, they set up assembly plants that used Chinese low-cost labour. It was, however, not a win-win situation for the West. The US kept complaining that an artificially pegged currency does not offer a level-playing field.

On the other hand, in the 1990s, India had relaxed its foreign exchange controls, beginning with trade on current account. This enabled India to align itself with international practices. The rupee consequently became a floating currency pegged to a basket of international currencies.

The question arises about the connection of this narrative with the equilibrium of the firm. For this purpose, we can do an initial examination of a product to be manufactured. There is hardly any product not based on the assembly of different components ranging from automobiles, which use over 10,000 components, to computers, televisions, home appliances, machinery, and defence equipment; even the humble pen is an assembly of different components. Each component or sub-assembly, furthermore, is produced by a firm of medium or large size to meet the requirements of end users from whom they derive their demand. For instance, Sona Steering in India is a big firm that supplies steering systems to a large number of automobile manufacturers. About five foundries supply engine blocks and heads for all the cars, tractors, and trucks made in the country. The myriad components cannot even be included in a single list. International trade comprises not just the finished goods and services but also components and sub-assemblies.

This is indeed a far cry from Smith's pin factory that used labour, simple hand tools, and an input-like wire. Even Marshall envisioned a homogenous end product while Robinson and Chamberlin modified it by introducing the notion of product differentiation.

Equilibrium analysis in the global setting, however, involves a number of steps. First, the firm needs to estimate the domestic and foreign demand for its product over a given period of time. It would then lay out its investment programme with respect to: (a) what quantity to manufacture, (b) what to manufacture in-house, (c) what to procure from local sources, and (d) what to import. Such a plan would normally be governed by the quality and extent of the local infrastructure—more specifically the presence of ancillaries and the complexity of the components proposed to be manufactured.

Generally, the more complex a component, the more likely that its manufacture would be deferred in view of higher investment or a longer learning period. Consequently, the product, at any stage of manufacture, would be a collection of domestic and imported components assembled in the desired manner. The relative weightage of the domestic and imported components would then determine the level of import substitution. The foreign exchange value of the imported parts, however, would have to be weighed by the exchange rate to bring them on a common scale. Thus, import substitution can be defined as the ratio of the foreign exchange value of the imported components in a product, substituted by components produced or procured indigenously by the firm, to the total foreign exchange value of that product. This means that the components that are procured indigenously and contain an imported element would be treated as wholly indigenous since they are paid for in the domestic currency by the procuring firm. On the other hand, they would feature in the import substitution programme of the supplier firm.

In Figure 1, one can observe that the replacement of imported components by indigenous components takes place in various stages. Each stage could represent a higher level of investment or technology. As the import content in terms of foreign exchange drops, the indigenous content in terms of foreign exchange replacement value goes up correspondingly. The indigenous content measured in domestic currency, of course, bears no relation to its imported counterpart since that will depend on domestic

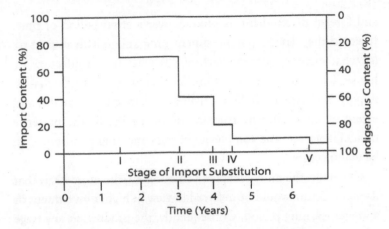

Figure 1 Stages of Import Substitution over Time

Source: Bharat-Ram (1997: 35).

cost parameters. Once the entire imported product is substituted by domestic value added, given the exchange rate, its cost is expected to be lower than that of the imported one. However, this need not always be true, the case of defence equipment being an example. Defence equipment is indigenized for strategic reasons. For commercial firms, it depends on various factors, including the stage at which the profit is maximum. Stages I, II, III, IV, and V, furthermore, do not have to be equal in duration, as seen on the timescale. For instance, it takes eighteen months to reduce the import content by 25 per cent in stage I. Cumulatively, stage II will bring the import content down by 60 per cent in three years, stage III by 80 per cent in four years, stage IV by 90 per cent in four-and-a-half years and, finally, stage V will bring the total import content down by 95 per cent in six-and-a-half years from the time of commencement.

This pattern is roughly equivalent to the time it took for the first Maruti car to be indigenized in the 1980s. Thereafter, for later models, the time frame was compressed because of experience and the fuller use of the existing equipment. The sequence proceeds along the following stages:

1. A shed has to be put up after the land is acquired for final
    assembly and inspection.

*A student, visibly flustered, asks, 'But why? The car has not been
manufactured yet, so how can you inspect it?'*

It is a good point. In fact, import substitution moves backwards.
Initially, kits are imported in a 'knock down' condition, which
means crates containing body parts, the engine, the power train,
the steering system, wheels, break system, and so on. The idea is
to reassemble these parts and check the vehicle for quality. This
by itself is a complex process. A lot of skill and learning go into
assembling a car, and with time, the efficiency and productivity of
the workers go up.

2. The next stage is welding and painting. Welding is required
    because each body part is sent separately, probably packed in
    lots of a dozen each. These parts have to be welded together
    in accordance with a detailed plan with welding equipment,
    which may be imported or domestically acquired. Once
    done, the shell of the car is ready for painting. This takes
    place in special booths with fairly sophisticated equipment.
3. Next comes the pressing of body parts, which requires
    high-powered presses and special dyes. This is an expensive
    process that involves costly equipment. The dyes are mostly
    imported, whereas the presses, though imported in the
    beginning, could be outsourced to specialized ancillaries
    over time.
4. This is followed by the machining of engine components
    and the assembly of the engine. After rigorous testing the
    engine is ready for use.
5. This stage involves the power train with the assembly of the
    gear box, by which time the vehicle nears completion.

Supporting the aforementioned stages is a whole range of ancillaries. For example, there is rather high investment process of casting of engine, blocks, heads, and housings, which requires a foundry. This is normally set up by external manufacturers who supply the required items to a cluster of vehicle manufacturers.

Running parallel with the assembly process are a host of smaller items required, like headlights, batteries, locks, wipers, air-conditioning systems, music systems, and so on, which are either farmed out to local manufacturers or imported. It is important to note that even when ancillaries for all items exist, some may be imported considering the cost and/or quality. For example, Indian foundries are in competition with Chinese foundries for the supply of castings to our own auto industry. Likewise, Mexican foundries compete with Indian foundries for supplies to American automakers. Such is the case with our whole chain of ancillaries.

'What about other industries like household appliances?' a student inquires.

I purposely picked the example of the auto industry because it produces arguably the most complex of consumer goods. Most other products follow a similar pattern.

It should be noted here that as an economy matures, the number of steps of import substitution tend to become fewer. Firms have the capital and experience to, say, invest in engine machining and the building of the power train at one go. On the other hand, they could outsource to either local ancillaries or import.

In terms of planning for the future, a firm would create a box diagram of its import substitution possibilities based on technical parameters, which follows a step function as shown earlier. Having chosen a stage of import substitution given the exchange rate, the firm then addresses the question of how much it should produce based on its demand curve, its fixed costs, and its variable costs in order to maximize profit. This should be straightforward as also shown in the previous chapter. However, in the global setting we find that we have two demand curves, one for the domestic market and another for the export market (assuming we consider all foreign markets as one). In addition, we have two kinds of fixed costs: one based on domestic capital assets and the other on imported ones. Similarly, we have two kinds of variable costs: one based on domestic and the other on imported items. Finally, if the exchange rate changes, the export demand function and both the imported fixed and variable costs will also change. Thus how can the equilibrium be determined?

The following steps are involved in reaching equilibrium.

For a given exchange rate (X) and a given stage of import substitution, we have to determine the total quantity of production (Q) and how much to sell in the domestic market (Q_d) and in the global market (Q_g) assuming there is no build-up of stock.

Revenue from the domestic market in domestic currency is

$$R_d = (A - BQ_d)(Q_d)$$

where the domestic average revenue curve is

$$A - BQ_d$$

Likewise, revenue from the global market in foreign currency is

$$R_g = (C - DQ_g)Q_g$$

where the average global revenue curve is

$$C - DQ_g$$

Thus total revenue R in domestic currency for Q is

$$R = R_d + R_g X$$

Having determined the revenue, we now have to arrive at the cost given the stage of import substitution for the aforementioned quantity. We thus need to put together the following elements of cost.

VC_d is the domestic variable cost, VC_g the imported variable cost in foreign currency, and $VC_d + VC_g X$ is the total variable cost in domestic currency. Likewise, FC_d is the domestic fixed cost, FC_g the imported fixed cost in foreign currency, and $FC_d + FC_g\, X$ is the fixed cost in domestic currency.

Thus total cost in domestic currency is

$$C = (VC_d + VC_g X) + (FC_d + FC_g\, X)$$

and profit $(\pi) = R - C$

$$= (R_d + R_g X) - [(VC_d + VC_g\, X) + FC_d + FC_g\, X)] \tag{1}$$

$$= R_d(Q_d) + R_g(Q_g)\, X - [(VC_d(Q) + VC_g(Q)\, X) + FC_d(Q) + FC_g(Q)\, X)] \tag{2}$$

$$= R_d(Q_d) + R_g(Q - Q_d)\, X - [(VC_d(Q) + VC_g(Q)\, X) + FC_d(Q) + FC_g(Q)X)] \tag{3}$$

$$(\therefore Q_g = Q - Q_d)$$

For maximizing π

$$\frac{\partial \pi}{\partial Q} = 0$$

and $\dfrac{\partial \pi}{\partial Qd} = 0$

Values of Q and Q_d are obtained from equations (2) and (3), and the value of Q_g is equal to $Q - Q_d$.

'Cool,' I heard a voice say.

'Not yet,' I said. How do we know this is the point of maximum profit? We have not so far determined the optimum stage of import substitution for a given exchange rate.

Equations (2) and (3) tell us that we have two average revenue curves, and that the fixed and variable costs will result in a U-shaped average total cost curve as explained in the previous chapter. Their difference shows that total profits go up gradually and then come down, thus indicating the point of maximum profit where the slope of the profit curve is zero.

a given exchange rate, say (X) rupees to a US dollar, Figure 2 shows
the stage of maximum profit.

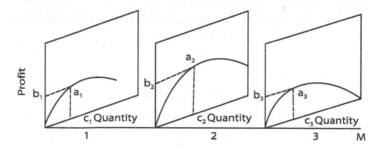

Figure 2   Stage 2 Shows the Highest Profit

Source: Bharat-Ram (1982: 34).

If, however, the exchange rate depreciates to $(X + \Delta X)$ rupees to
a dollar, the profits will shift in all three diagrams and the maximum profit will be at stage 3 of Figure 3.

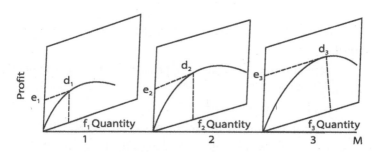

Figure 3   Stage 3 Shows the Highest Profit

Source: Bharat-Ram (1982: 34).

This makes intuitive sense since a depreciated rupee will make
imports more expensive and it will also push the firm towards
greater import substitution. Likewise, if the rupee appreciates, the
tendency will be to reduce the latter.

So what we now have is an equilibrium that tells us the total quantity to produce, how much of that to sell in the domestic market, how much to export, and at what level of import substitution to stop, given the exchange rate.

Thus we can conclude that we have a model for the global firm.[3]

❧

Nevertheless, there is another area of analysis that comes under both microeconomics and macroeconomics—the production function that was originally developed by Charles Cobb and Paul Douglas in 1928. The production function is now famous as the Cobb–Douglas production function and its standard formulation is:

$$Y = AK^{\alpha} L^{\beta}$$

where

Y = total production (the real value of all goods produced in a year),

L = labour input (the total number of person-hours worked in a year),

K = capital input (the real value of all machinery, equipment, and buildings), and

A = total factor productivity.

α and β are the output elasticities of capital and labour respectively. These values are constants determined by the available technology.

---

[3] Numerous case studies and simulations have shown that this model is quite robust in the sense that small changes in the exchange rate do not affect the desired stage of import substitution. See Vinay Bharat-Ram's *The Theory of the Global Firm* (1997).

Output elasticity measures the responsiveness of output to a change in levels of either labour or capital used in production with other factors remaining the same. For example, if $\alpha = 0.50$, a 1 per cent increase in capital usage would lead to approximately a 0.50 per cent increase in output. Further, if α and β add up to one, we have a case of constant returns; if they add up to less than one, we have diminishing returns, and if they add up to more than one, we have increasing returns.

This function has been used for decades by economists after Douglas applied it to US census data and established its reliability. Nevertheless, it has always been applied within economies and not to trade between countries. I will, therefore, suggest a different formulation.

For the purpose of illustration, let us take the example of the Cincinnati Milacron CNC flexible system made in the US for machining automobile cylinder blocks and the similar HMT system made in India. Here,

$$P_m = XP^*$$

where P_m is the domestic price of the imported system determined by its foreign currency price P^* times the nominal exchange rate X. The difference of the two systems, however, is based on objective considerations of relative productivity-cum-price. The US system produces, say, twice the number of engine blocks per unit of time as compared to the Indian system. Therefore, if the price of the Indian system is greater than half that of the US system, it will be less cost-effective; it will be more if the price is less than half that of the US system.

If this example of investment goods procured from domestic and foreign sources, meant for the same end purpose, were aggregated for the whole economy, $PI_d + P_m I_m$ would equal the size of total investment, where P is the average price of domestic investment goods I_d and P_m the average price of imported investment goods I_m.

Since output Q is related to aggregate investment, that is, I_d and I_m, this relationship may be expressed in the Cobb–Douglas form as a production function.

$$Q = \mu \, I^{\alpha}_{d \, (P'} \, I_m)^{\beta}$$

where $P'(= P_m/P)$ is the price of imported investments goods in relation to the price of domestic investment goods that serve the same end purpose,

α is the elasticity of aggregate output with respect to domestic investment goods,

and β with respect to imported investment goods.

Furthermore, if K is the marginal productivity of both domestic and imported investment goods I_d and I_m, then

$$K = K_d + K_m$$

where K_d and K_m are the marginal productivities of domestic and imported investment goods respectively.

$$K_d = \frac{\partial Q}{\partial I_d}$$
$$= \mu \alpha I_d^{\alpha-1} (P' I_m)^{\beta}$$
$$K_m = \frac{\partial Q}{\partial (P' I_m)}$$
$$= \mu \beta I_d^{\alpha} (P' I_m)^{\beta-1}$$

The marginal rate of substitution (M_{RS}) of imported investment goods by domestic investment goods

$$= K_m / K_d$$
$$= \frac{\mu \beta I_d^{\alpha} (P' I_m)^{\beta-1}}{\mu \alpha I_d^{\alpha-1} (P' I_m)^{\beta}}$$
$$= \frac{\beta I_d}{\alpha P' I_m}$$
$$= \frac{\beta P I_d}{\alpha P_m I_m} = \frac{\beta P I_d}{\alpha X P^* I_m}$$

It may be noted that when the exchange rate X depreciates given α and β, or α rises in relation to β given X, I_m will be substituted by I_d in the expression $\beta PI_d / \alpha XP^* I_m$, thus raising the M_{RS}. The converse will also be true.

Over time, with technical progress through technology transfer, import substitution, and learning, it is conceivable that the gap between α and β will narrow. Going back to our example of the Cincinnati versus the HMT systems, there will be an initial period of learning and familiarization by trial and error with the Indian substitute, which will take time to reach its rated productivity level. Thereafter, there are various ways in which HMT can copy or adapt, say, the computer-aided design (CAD) or computer-aided manufacturing (CAM) features of the Cincinnati system, thus raising its output per unit of time.

This brings us to the importance of innovation through copying superior technologies and then improving upon them. The transistor, for example, was invented in the US. However, Sony of Japan not only copied it but also miniaturized it, thus creating a whole chain of new products. Likewise, Tata of India created the cheapest car in the world using a combination of imported technology and innovation.

⚭

We shall now move to the subject of entrepreneurship and innovation, which takes us more than a century back to the ideas of Schumpeter.

Entrepreneurship and Innovation

Joseph Alois Schumpeter (1883–1950) was a fascinating man who straddled two world views with regard to economic development. The first was influenced by the intellectual climate in the late nineteenth century—particularly of the Austrian school, though he was well-acquainted with Marx as well as neoclassical economics originating from Britain (Jevons and Marshall) and France (Walras). Schumpeter graduated in law from the University of Vienna and then studied political economy under the eminent theorist Eugen von Böhm-Bawerk, completing his PhD in 1906. Thereafter, he wrote his famous *The Theory of Economic Development*, which was published in 1912 in German and in 1934 in English. It presented his preliminary world view, while his equally famous *Capitalism, Socialism and Democracy* (1942) expressed his final, evolved world view.

The period before the First World War, though one of rapid growth, was characterized by business cycles of varying duration, so to speak, contained within the Kondratiev wave of forty-five to sixty years. Marx referred to the capitalist system as inherently prone to periodic crises. Schumpeter added to this his own historical experience of rapid industrial growth in Europe in the late nineteenth and early twentieth centuries where, despite booms and crises, the overall levels of prosperity and economic development were unprecedented.

Schumpeter's *The Theory of Economic Development* sets out to explain this phenomenon in terms of innovations, innovativeness, and entrepreneurship.[1]

Although economic development as understood today refers to the Third World countries, this was not the focus of Schumpeter's book. He was concerned with the development of capitalism in the industrialized world. To this end, he began by describing received equilibrium theory, which he called 'static' or 'comparative static' and contrasted it with 'dynamic'. The latter, he argued, was the force behind real economic development as distinguished from mere economic growth, which emanates from the *circular flow of economic life as conditioned by given circumstances*. This would be the case in a stationary state of general equilibrium where the circular flow would ensure that demand matches supply and individuals as consumers or suppliers maximize their monetary gains at the point of equilibrium. Market demand determines the allocation of resources and the money value of their respective marginal products determines the income. Economic stability and full employment are ensured by equilibrium in the money market as well as the market for all assets and labour. Schumpeter believed that under such conditions the role of money would be marginalized, a point that was objected to by his Austrian compatriots.

The thrust of Schumpeter's argument nevertheless was that the economy would grow along a predictable equilibrium path based on increases in population, labour, savings, capital accumulation, and changes in consumer tastes. One may ask where, in such a

[1] See Ulrich Witt's 2002 article 'How Evolutionary Is Schumpeter's Theory of Economic Development?'.

passive state of equilibrium, would be the need for leaders with foresight, vision, and the innovative spirit.

The circular flow argument, even though a somewhat artificial construct, became a perfect launching pad for Schumpeter's 'innovator entrepreneur' as the driving force behind economic development. Further, development was characterized not by a mere response to changes in external data but a process of evolution from within the economic system, which displaces old equilibria and creates a movement towards higher growth. Behind such changes is Schumpeter's 'heroic' figure of the entrepreneur who—as cited in John Elliot's introduction to The Theory of Economic Development—has 'the drive and the will to found a private kingdom'; to fight for the joy of combat rather than for immediate financial gain; take risks and build new products; find new ways of doing things; combine the same factors in unprecedented ways; invest in 'roundabout methods' of production, a concept borrowed from Böhm-Bawerk; to raise productivity and reduce costs; and in the process create a perennial gale of creative destruction. By this, he meant the periodic replacement of the existing methods of production and the disruption of the existing positions of equilibrium.

Schumpeter acknowledged that people who fit into this heroic figure of an entrepreneur are rare in society. Nevertheless, according to him, a 'swarm' of imitators follows each innovation or set of innovations, with interesting consequences. First, the innovator makes large extra-normal profits until the point at which the imitators catch up. Unless intellectual property rights protect such profits, as they do in today's world, they are eventually wiped out and the wait begins for a new cycle of innovations. This was much the case as Schumpeter saw it. Moreover, Schumpeter argued that while the innovator makes extra-normal profits, he brings about a general rise in the level of economic prosperity and touches off a cyclical boom. Such a boom, however, is invariably followed by a slump once the imitators have crowded out extra-normal profits by, say, overinvestment in now-known processes, and further, banks who have over-extended credit at the tail end of the boom only exacerbate the downswing of the cycle.

'But why do innovations have to be cyclical?' a student wants to know.

Schumpeter himself gave the best answer to this: this is so because innovations or new combinations are not—as one would expect according to the general principles of probability—evenly distributed through time, but appear, if at all, discontinuously in groups or swarms. What follows thus is that economic develop-ment takes place because of bursts of innovative investments, which are accompanied by new technologies, organizational changes, and rising productivity. The bunching of innovations is therefore as much a cause of prosperity as of depression. In other words, if you want the former, you must accept the latter. With the onset of the Great Depression of the 1930s, Schumpeter is believed to have once told his class at Harvard that a depression was nothing more serious than a cold 'douche'. Of course, to the question of how long this could last, he gave a general answer. As to short-term depressions, which we call recessions today, Schumpeter believed that they encourage cost-cutting, raising of productivity, and the elimination of waste. This readies firms for the next upswing. Long-term depressions, according to him, were beyond the pale of rational thinking where pathological factors like 'panic' or 'crises' take over and it becomes difficult to predict their duration.

Schumpeter is also famous for his work on business cycles. He came out with his masterly work titled *Business Cycles: A Theoretical, Historical and Statistical Analysis of the Capitalist Process* in 1939. Alas, its publication coincided with the Great Depression, which had wrought untold misery on the industrial nations—a point when the focus was on looking for solutions rather than analyses of the ongoing problem. In terms of timing, Keynes had provided an answer in his *General Theory of Employment, Interest and Money* (1936), as we shall discuss later. For now, let us note that the cyclic theory was no longer the flavour of the day and it is not hard to imagine the disdain in which Schumpeter held Keynes. Incidentally, Schumpeter and Keynes shared the same year of birth—1883—the year that also marked the end of Marx's life.

Before we move on to Schumpeter's final world view, some anecdotes about him. Paul McCracken, the economic advisor to the US President Dwight D. Eisenhower in the mid-1950s, was our professor at Ann Arbor, Michigan. He had studied under Schumpeter at Harvard in the 1930s and described the first class he attended. Schumpeter would wait for the class to be in full attendance. He would then make a dramatic entry, taking off his hat, gloves, and the European-style cloak with a flourish before launching forth in his Viennese-accented English. His favourite line was that he wanted to be the greatest economist, the greatest equestrian, and the greatest lover; and that he had accomplished two of his ambitions. He never said which two.

Rounding off Schumpeter's first world view, we must note that he defended capitalism against two major criticisms: a) that it created monopolies and b) that it led to inequalities of incomes. About the first, he acknowledged that monopolies did lead to extra-normal profits but that they were a just reward for the uncertainties surrounding innovation. Further, competition would wipe out these rewards, but the new technologies and quality improvements were there to stay. Additionally, competition may eliminate extra-normal profits but innovation will recreate them and so the cycle will go on. In Schumpeter's own words, surplus values [extra-normal profits] may be impossible in perfect equilibrium but can be ever present because that equilibrium is never allowed to establish itself. They may always tend to vanish and yet be always there because they are constantly recreated.

On the point about inequalities of income, Schumpeter believed that capitalism brings in mass production, which lowers costs and prices to the greater benefit of the common man. Further, while relative poverty (inequality of incomes) may be a necessary condition of capitalism, absolute poverty is not. In other words, as capitalism lifts the general level of prosperity, absolute poverty should also decline.

'How can you say that? In India we have so much poverty despite capitalism.'

That is a loaded question. The inequalities that capitalism has brought about are like between Mukesh Ambani's annual income of Rs 240 million and that of a medium-size entrepreneur earning, say, Rs 10 million a year. This does not hurt despite the huge gap. Then there are those who make only Rs 5,000 a month. It hurts, but not as much as for those who are unemployed and have no means of sustenance. Schumpeter would probably have said that over time dynamic capitalism has improved the condition of the poor. Nevertheless, he provided us with no clear answer. On the other hand, since the reforms of 1990-1 the poverty index has undeniably improved in India.

Schumpeter, upon getting a position at Harvard in 1932, migrated from Europe to America for good. It was the beginning of the Great Depression and the rise of Hitler in Germany. By the time the war preparations were in full swing in the US towards the end of the 1930s, the depression had lifted and US industry had come to the fore with a series of new inventions and innovations in the chemical and engineering industries to support the defence effort. In the aftermath of the war, these innovations gave an impetus to the rise of large corporations like DuPont, General Motors, and IBM. Schumpeter's *Capitalism, Socialism and Democracy* reflected these developments and inspired his grand vision of the future of capitalism. The opening chapters are devoted to Marx's many-sided personality as a social scientist and his concept of historical materialism. Taking inspiration from the latter, Schumpeter declared that the promoter–innovator–entrepreneur was now obsolete and that future innovations would take place within the bureaucratic structure of large corporations.

Monopolies would emerge, but competition from other large corporations would eliminate them. In other words, the perennial gale of creative destruction would continue to prevail.

To many the fading away of the innovator-entrepreneur may come as a surprise. However, it was for real—a consequence of the spawning of the large corporation, the need for large amounts of risk capital, and the departmentalization of research and development.

The bigger surprise, however, was yet to come. Schumpeter believed that much as he was opposed to socialism, the days of capitalism were numbered; that the capitalist order tends to destroy itself and the centralist socialism is ... a likely heir apparent, as cited by Skousen in his *The Making of Modern Economics*. He believed that society would much prefer stability to the unpredictability of capitalism, and that socialism was capable of delivering this. In short, socialism would not enter through the front door as Marx had predicted, but through the back door of capitalist enterprise.

What, in effect, is our assessment of Schumpeter? He was, without doubt, an eclectic thinker and his two world views have inspired two very different kinds of readership. The first was hailed as inspirational in business schools and by the capitalist world in general. The economics profession, however, distanced itself since equilibrium analysis has continued to dominate economic thinking. The socialists, on the other hand, found much to admire in Schumpeter's second world view, despite the entry of socialism through the back door. Considering the time when Schumpeter wrote his second world view, he seemed to be in thrall of Marx and Marxism. The capitalist would have gone through the trauma of the Great Depression while the Soviet Union with its monolithic public sector industries had been able to avoid mass unemployment and provide stability to the economic system. Hence the lure of socialism. It is ironic that while his contemporary Keynes fought to protect capitalism from socialism, Schumpeter succumbed to it.

For the modern reader, however, there are many later developments to ponder on—such as the collapse of the Soviet Union and the spread of capitalism in a globalized world as well as a plethora of young innovators–entrepreneurs, especially in the information technology-related industries in the late twentieth and twenty-first centuries—which have challenged the might of the large corporation.

Money Matters

By the twentieth century, microeconomics seemed to be on a firm footing. Marshall's concepts of supply and demand based on the marginalist revolution as well as equilibrium analysis were a standard part of the economics curriculum in colleges. Macroeconomics, too, was fairly common knowledge going back to Smith's notions of liberalism, capital accumulation, and thrift as the conditions for maximizing the wealth of nations. Added to this, J.B. Say's law, according to which supply creates its own demand, completed the circle. In other words, the wages earned through production would necessarily be spent on the fruits of production and the occasional mismatch between demand and supply—that was believed to be the cause of a recession—would eventually correct itself.

What remained to be discovered in the field of economics?

'Money,' *a few in the classroom spoke in unison.*

Quite right. But what is money?

As we noted earlier, during the mercantile era, gold and silver were the standard measures of wealth. Smith, of course, disagreed, as according to him, the volume of trade between individuals and countries accounted for real wealth, and gold and silver were merely a medium of exchange. It was more than a century after Smith that the great American economist Irving Fisher (1867–1947) focused on the study of money.

 83

MONEY MATTERS

National currencies were originally measured in specific weights of gold or silver. For instance, in the middle ages, the British pound was worth a pound of sterling silver. Likewise, other currencies like the American dollar and German mark were based on gold or silver. Smith, however, favoured the gold standard for international trade and this endured until the First World War. If a country's aggregate exports exceeded its imports, the difference was settled in gold. In consequence, if gold flowed into a country, this frequently resulted in inflation and boom conditions. Thereafter, if export prices rose, a fall in exports and an excess of imports could lead to slump conditions. In other words, the gold standard was not a perfect mechanism. The gold rush in California and new discoveries of gold in Australia and South Africa further exacerbated the problem of adhering to a gold standard. The boom and bust cycle about which we talked in the chapters on Marx and Schumpeter continued well into the twentieth century.

On the other hand, with the growth of trade in the eighteenth and nineteenth centuries, promissory notes—or the promise to pay—had become commonplace. These were nothing but paper money that could be redeemed in gold or silver. The redeeming gradually became the responsibility of banks, which could issue notes against deposits of gold and silver. The way it worked was that those with surplus gold or silver could deposit it with a bank and earn a small interest, while those who needed money for transactions could be issued paper money by the bank at a higher interest rate. This was a wonderful system so long as the banks maintained a credible ratio of hard cash, in gold and silver to the loans given out. This was easier said than done, especially in the newly independent British colonies in America. Private banks were now free to issue money to friends, associates, and the owners. For a while it seemed, as Galbraith puts it in his *The Age of Uncertainty*, the citizens of the new republic discovered banking as an adolescent discovers sex. The power to print money was indeed a heady intoxicant. Equally sobering was the hangover of bankruptcy.

'Was Galbraith always so funny?' a student wants to know.

He truly was—as goes the story. Someone had once asked Galbraith why he never used mathematics in his writings. Pat had come the response that only those who did not have a grasp on the English language used mathematics. Galbraith seldom missed an opportunity to have a dig at the economics profession—especially of the Chicago school of thought. We shall come back to him later.

The history of banking is chequered and interspersed with booms, busts, inflation, and bank failures. In the end, countries realized the need for a central bank to discipline the commercial banks and bring some order. Britain was the first to establish the Bank of England, which was a marvellous institution. It brought stability and prestige to the pound sterling. The US established the Federal Reserve System in 1913, just prior to the war.

This brings us to Fisher who is often called the father of the monetarist school.

Born in upstate New York, Fisher graduated from Yale College in 1889 and continued his doctoral work in mathematical economics. His dissertation 'Mathematical Investigations in the Theory of Value and Price' (1892) was hailed as pioneering by Samuelson.

At a young age, Fisher was diagnosed with tuberculosis—a disease regarded as deadly in those times. However, he survived it through outdoor living, a simple diet, and plenty of exercise. He wore stylish clothes and had a moustache and short beard. A many-sided personality, in addition to being a prolific writer on money and index numbers, he demonstrated that he could also make money. He did so by inventing an index card system, which was later patented as the Rolodex. In the following years, he became a millionaire.

By the arrival of the Roaring Twenties, Fisher could be seen smiling—a marked change in demeanour from his earlier serious visage. Was it money that brought about this change? It could have, as money surely can do wonders.

'What were the Roaring Twenties?' a student asked.

The best way to get a feel of the 1920s is to read F. Scott Fitzgerald's *The Great Gatsby*—or, for that matter, to see the film released in 2013 under the same title. The 1920s were a time when growing affluence was visible in the lifestyle of the citizens. The stock market was on the upswing, industrial investment was high, and prices were stable.

This was also a time when Fisher was riding high not just on his millions but also as the 'Oracle of Wall Street'. Fisher was bullish about the future. His optimism was not based on mere sentiment; its foundation lay in the Quantity Theory of Money,[1] his key contribution to monetary economics.

This was expressed as a mathematical equation that is shown below:

$$M \times V = P \times Q$$

where M is the total stock or quantity of money in circulation and V is the velocity of circulation or the number of times in a year that cash plus bank deposits change hands. For example, if the quantity of money supply is USD 500 billion and it circulates six times in a year, then the total value of all the transactions of goods and services will equal USD 3 trillion.

On the other side of the equation, P is the general price level and Q the total quantity of goods and services transacted during a year. In a sense, the equation is true by definition; it is tautology.

Fisher, however, regarded this equation as a theory. He believed that so long as the price level P remained stable, there was no

---

[1] The theory was published in Fisher's *The Purchasing Power of Money* (2012).

reason to worry about a boom or a slump. A number of eminent economists, including Keynes, shared his belief. Nevertheless, two equally eminent economists of the neo-Austrian school, Ludwig von Mises (1881–1973) and Friedrich von Hayek (1899–1992), believed that Fisher's theory was flawed. Regrettably, Mises, the senior of the two, who had predicted a major crash in his *The Theory of Money and Credit* (1912), went unnoticed in the English-speaking world as his book was translated only in 1934, much after the Wall Street crash of 1929. Hayek as director of the Austrian Institute of Economic Research, too, made an amazingly accurate prediction. Both Mises and Hayek believed that while Fisher's equation was right, he should have focused on M rather than P. In other words, a policy of easy money by the Federal Reserve was the culprit and watching the price level alone was misleading.

Fisher's theory actually hid some rather dangerous assumptions. Price stability implied that money is neutral or simply a veil over the real economy and that if more money is issued, prices will rise proportionately in every sector of industry. The assumption that V and Q would remain stable was hardly credible. Further, prices, especially in the capital goods sector with a long gestation period vary considerably from those in the consumer goods sectors. The belief implicit here was that capital was like a homogenous fund that could be transferred from one sector to another and that if adjustments were required they would be of a short-term nature and things would be back to normal. In short, Fisher focused on long-term macroeconomic stability rather than on possible crises emerging in the short term.

Throughout most of the 1920s, prices were stable and the Federal Reserve followed a policy of low interest rates and easy credit, little realizing that a huge amount of money was going into capital expansion, housing, and real estate. A steady rise in share prices on the New York Stock Exchange reflected this.

The Wall Street crash of October 1929 was without doubt the greatest financial calamity of the twentieth century. The ever-optimist Fisher lost his entire fortune, faced bankruptcy, and died a miserable man. His contribution to monetary theory, however, lives on at the Chicago School.

'So what really happened?' a student asks.

Well, numerous books and PhD dissertations have been written on this question. In fact, Galbraith's *The Great Crash 1929* (2009) became a bestseller. The sales were, however, low at airport bookstalls!

◈

The next chapter attempts a thumbnail sketch of the events and the causes leading up to the crash. And we talk about the ideas of Keynes.

The Saviour of Capitalism

First came the crash—then the Great Depression. Between 1929 and 1933, in America the unemployment rate rose to 25 per cent, almost half the commercial banks failed, industrial production dropped by more than 30 per cent, and shares lost nearly 90 per cent of their value. The crisis spread to Europe and indeed to all free market economies. Soviet Russia, a full-fledged socialist country, was spared the brunt of the problem.

It was not the best of times for free market economists. They could only come up with clichéd advice like belt tightening, the need for balanced budgets, patience, and that like other business cycles this, too, shall pass. A quote by Keynes in often cited where he says, 'Economists set themselves too easy, too useless a task if in tempestuous seasons they can tell us that when the storm is long past the ocean is flat again.' This tempest lasted a full decade.

For the Marxists and Socialists the times were rather celebratory. They saw the end of capitalism unfolding before them, especially as the depression wore on with no end in sight. The establishment began to doubt the robustness of the capitalist system and even the citadel of high theory, the London School of Economics (LSE)—under the leadership of Lionel Robbins and with Hayek as a professor—could come up with no solution. Hayek, in fact, had been invited by Robbins to create a counterforce to the growing popularity of Keynes at Cambridge.

'But who was Keynes? You have referred to him so often,' a student asked.

John Maynard Keynes (1883–1946) was born in a family of intellectuals. His father John Neville Keynes was an Economics Fellow at Cambridge University and his mother Florence Ada Keynes went on to become the mayor of Cambridge in later years. Maynard, as he was known to friends, attended the elite school known as Eton College and thereafter graduated in mathematics from King's College, Cambridge, in 1905. Keynes, by all accounts, had a remarkably happy childhood and throughout his life suffered from no personal discontent. In contrast was Marx whose life ended in what was the year of birth for Keynes. As Galbraith mentions in his *The Age of Uncertainty*, 'Marx swore that the bourgeoisie would suffer for his poverty and his carbuncles. Keynes experienced neither poverty nor boils.' Keynes later got interested in economics under the influence of Marshall.

While at college, Keynes joined a group of young intellectuals who called themselves Apostles. Many members of this group were also associated with the Bloomsbury Group and met regularly in London. They were, in a sense, rebels against the conservative, staid Victorian values of the time. Comprising Lytton Strachey, Leonard and Virginia Woolf, Clive and Vanessa Bell, among other friends and lovers, they were greatly influenced by the philosopher G.E. Moore. Earlier members of the Apostles had been Alfred Lord Tennyson, Bertrand Russell, Alfred North Whitehead, and Moore himself. Perhaps influenced by the tenets of Greek philosophy, which held that love between males is spiritually more evolved than that between a man and a woman, Keynes was for some years a self-confessed homosexual. This, however, was to change when he married the beautiful Russian ballerina Lydia

Lopokova. According to *The Essential Galbraith*, this prompted the couplet:

'Was there ever such a union of beauty and brains
As when the lovely Lopokova married John Maynard Keynes'

Soon after college, Keynes sat for the civil service examinations. He did poorly in economics, which in his characteristic style he attributed to a lack of knowledge of the subject on the part of the examiner. As a civil servant, Keynes spent time at the India office where he wrote on Indian currency and probability theory. Shortly afterwards, he became a teaching fellow at Cambridge and the editor of Cambridge's famed *Economic Journal*. He went on to hold this position for more than three decades.

The turning point in Keynes's career was to arrive soon. With the advent of the Great War, the British Treasury required him to raise funds for the war effort. He did this by requisitioning earnings from trade, floating loans in the US, and commandeering securities for sale abroad. He was undoubtedly resourceful.

Post-war, in 1919 Keynes became a member of the British delegation to the Peace Conference at Versailles and technical advisor to British Prime Minister David Lloyd George. As the discussions went forward, Keynes became increasingly disillusioned. He resigned a few months later and returned to England to write what became a classic polemic titled *The Economic Consequences of the Peace* (1919).

Keynes's disillusionment proceeded on two fronts. First, the sheer immorality on the part of the victors—Georges Clemenceau of France, Woodrow Wilson of America, and Lloyd George of Britain—to write into the terms of the Armistice, which had just been concluded, further concessions of territory and gold that would end up beggaring Germany and impose greater suffering on women, children, and the aged who had little to do with the war. The Allies, particularly France, were in a spirit of vengeance, which led to Keynes's acid-laden but highly readable character sketches of the leaders. Keynes's arguments were by no means just emotional. He accounts in detail for a monetary figure of the reparations, which would be reasonable for both victor and vanquished and would not drive Germany to the wall where it would be forced to renege. His fears proved true.

The second argument—included in the opening chapter of *The Economic Consequences of the Peace*—speaks of the end of a civilization. Prior to 1914 there was a fragile but working structure of European civilization, which was based on the fact that those of average ability in the working class could slowly but surely improve their standard of living and that those in the capitalist class as per convention accumulated their earnings for future growth without wasting it on frivolous consumption. This structure had endured for half a century, but had come unstuck because of the war. According to Keynes, 'All classes alike thus build their plans, the rich to spend more and save less, the poor to spend more and work less.'

Indeed the world was changing. The close of the war marked the end of the Ottoman Empire (the movie *Lawrence of Arabia* depicts this), the birth of Palestine, the collapse of the Austro-Hungarian Empire, and the rise of the Soviet Union. At this moment in history when a new civilizational arrangement was in the making, Keynes warned against rash decisions—but to no avail. Many have attributed the rise of the Nazis to a vengeful France that forced ruinous reparations on Germany.

The Economic Consequences of the Peace became an instant bestseller much to the chagrin of the British establishment. It was exceedingly well-received by the intellectuals, especially in the US and Austria, including Schumpeter and Hayek.

A multifaceted personality, Keynes was a collector of paintings, a patron of the arts, bursar of King's College at Cambridge, chairman of the National Mutual Life Insurance Company, and a successful trader on the commodity and stock exchanges. He suffered heavy losses during the Great Depression but more than made up later becoming the richest economist after Ricardo.

The next brush with authority for Keynes came in 1925 when Winston Churchill as the Chancellor of the Exchequer returned the pound sterling to the gold standard at the pre-war fixed exchange rate, ignoring the fact that prices and wages had risen significantly during the years of the war. He seemed fixated on the pre-war world order; his 'finest hour' was to come during the Second World War. In his polemic *The Economic Consequences of Mr. Churchill* (1925), Keynes termed Churchill's decision as 'silly', as according to him it would lead to deflation and throw labour out of work unless wages were reduced. Furthermore, exports would be overpriced, thus leading to an outflow of gold.

In the two years that followed, gold did flow to the US at an alarming rate. This prompted Britain along with Germany and France to request the Federal Reserve to lower the interest rate, so that capital would stop moving into the US. The Federal Reserve obliged. This resulted in, as Galbraith explains in his *The Great Crash 1929*, easy money finding its way to the stock market, which sped up the imminent crash.

During the Depression, Keynes urged the authorities to follow a simple formula: borrow and spend. This was the only way out when the public sentiment weighed heavily in favour of thrift or a preference for liquidity and entrepreneurs were in no mood to invest. The government must spend on public works to create employment even if it meant deficit-financing. His advice was anti-budget-balancing and was anathema to the establishment and the prevailing economic wisdom, especially of the LSE.

Behind this scene, Adolf Hitler who had probably never heard of Keynes was doing just what he had recommended. He was borrowing and spending on autobahns and factories, building the Volkswagen and later armaments. Unemployment consequently disappeared by 1935. But Hitler was someone the free world would not deign to learn from.

At the beginning of 1935, Keynes told George Bernard Shaw, 'I believe myself to be writing a book which will largely revolutionize ... the way the world looks at economic problems', as Skousen cites in his *The Making of Modern Economics*. Keynes's *The General Theory of Employment, Interest and Money* was published in 1936 and was priced at just five shillings in order to make it affordable for students. Unlike his other writings, which were known for their prose and cadences, this book was acrostic. While highly critical of its style and tone, Samuelson nonetheless acclaimed it as 'a work of genius' in his *Foundations of Economic Analysis* (1983 [1947]). In the years to come, Samuelson and Alvin Hanson of Harvard were to make Keynes's ideas accessible to the economics profession.

'So was this book of practical importance during the Depression?' a student wants to know.

It certainly was of both practical and theoretical importance.

Keynes probably felt that his advice of 'borrow and spend' was not being taken seriously because it lacked a theoretical foundation. In his book, he advanced a theory that he felt stood on a solid foundation.

Some of Keynes's postulates sound rather obvious: that those who spend and those who invest are two different sets of people; that those who spend have a choice to either consume or save; and that those who invest have a choice to borrow the entire amount of saving or a part of it. In other words, since the investors and savers are different people, there is no reason why future saving and future investment will be equal. We shall examine the consequences.

'But what about past saving and investment?'

Past savings are always equal to past investment because investment is defined as the actual expenditure on fixed capital during, say, a year plus the difference in the opening and closing inventories. Since saving is income minus consumption, if the latter declines, inventories will rise and whatever is produced will not be fully consumed. In case consumption rises, this will work in the opposite direction, that is, inventories will be drawn down and investment will increase. Thus saving and investment are always equal.

Y (gross domestic product) = C (consumption) + I (investment)

What Keynes observed during the Great Depression was that both consumption and investment had declined and in consequence so had the GDP, which at factor cost is the sum of income from employment, gross profits of companies, gross surplus of public utilities, rent, less net stock appreciation, and net income from abroad.

Since consumers tended to save more in times of high unemployment and underutilized resources, this adversely affected the business sentiment or what Keynes called the 'animal spirits' of entrepreneurs. This was not a short-term phenomenon; it continued to drag on. Keynes recommended that the government should step in and invest in public works like schools, roads, and other infrastructure if need be through deficit-financing. This would create direct employment, which was the need of the hour. So important was the creation of direct employment that even wasteful expenditure like 'digging holes' and filling them up would be beneficial. He therefore extended the GDP formula to include government spending:

Y = C + I + G

In other words, if C and I were pulling down Y, G should step in and fill the gap without bothering about budget deficits. But how would such a heretical idea, which flew in the face of conventional wisdom like belt tightening and budget balancing, work?

This is where Keynes introduced his magic. He dismissed increasing the money supply and lowering the interest rate as a solution because businesses would not borrow at even close to zero interest when the investment outlook was bleak. Keynes called this the 'liquidity trap'.

Further, consumers would not part with their savings in difficult times even if a high interest rate was offered to them. This Keynes termed as 'liquidity preference'. With a monetary solution out of the window, the only alternative was government spending through fiscal policy changes like borrowing and reducing taxes.

'But how will government spending bring about the full employment?', *a student asks.*

This would be brought about through Keynes's magic formula based on the marginal propensity to consume and the multiplier.

Keynes believed that saving depends upon income rather than the interest rate offered for borrowing as expounded by Knut Wicksell in his *Interest and Prices: A Study of the Causes Regulating the Value of Money* (1936) and the Austrian School. Further, in aggregate terms there exists at any time a marginal propensity to consume, which implies the urge to spend a certain proportion of the income or conversely the urge to save a certain proportion. In his own words, Keynes defined the marginal propensity to consume in his *General Theory of Employment, Interest and Money* as 'how the next increment of output will have to be divided between consumption and investment'. He used this to explain his multiplier concept.[1]

Let us examine a case where the government plans to build a dam, the wage bill for which is Rs 10 billion. In consequence, this amount should go into the economy. Assume that the workers save 10 per cent of their income and spend the rest on necessities like food, clothing, children's education, rent, and so on. This means that their marginal propensity to consume is 90 per cent

---

[1] The employment multiplier—not the investment multiplier—was first proposed by Richard Kahn, Keynes's student. See Kahn's paper 'The Relation of Home Investment to Unemployment' (1931).

and that Rs 9 billion will move into the system. Again, if those who receive this money as income spend 90 per cent, the next round of income will be Rs 8.1 billion, and so on. Thus, with each round of spending, assuming the marginal propensity to consume remains the same and the incremental investment-to-employment ratio is constant, the initial dose of investment will lead to employment and investment that is ten times larger.[2] Keynes's formula for this was:

$$k = \frac{1}{1 - MPC}$$

where k is the multiplier and its value as we see from the above example is ten.

The implications of this discovery during the Depression were revolutionary. Here was an antidote for years of suffering of the unemployed and the capitalists who saw hope for the fuller utilization of resources. It was too good to be true and was received with scepticism within the British establishment. The LSE later regretted that it was slow in accepting the wisdom of Keynes.

Keynes later travelled to America and after a less-than-satisfactory meeting with President Franklin D. Roosevelt, he decided to sell his ideas to the universities starting with Harvard. He found a receptive audience especially among the young economists like Galbraith, Samuelson, and Alvin Hanson. They played a key role in explaining the General Theory to the academic world as well as the establishment in Washington, DC. Keynes, who was already a celebrity, reached the pinnacle of his career with the remarkable success of his General Theory.

This was, however, not an easy victory for Keynes. Since he had given the state such an important role in the recovery process, he was dubbed as anti-free market and left-leaning by the classical economists. Hayek, about whom we shall talk later, had to give in to the Keynesian solution but was never reconciled to it.

But what had Keynes said in essence? Keynes believed that capitalism left to itself was unstable like a car without a driver; that there was no reason to believe that equilibrium would necessarily be achieved at a level of full employment; that underemployment equilibrium was a distinct possibility and therefore the government must take hold of the steering wheel. What this meant was deficit-financing during recession but pulling back on spending and raising taxes if necessary once full employment was reached and inflation was rearing its head. A full-employment economy would ensure high revenues and wipe out budget deficits.

An example of underemployment equilibrium is illustrated in Figure 1:

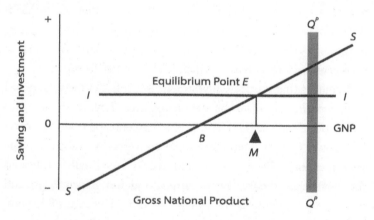

Figure 1 How Savings and Investments Determine Income

Source: Samuelson and Nordhaus (1992 [1948]).

Note: The equilibrium level of national output is determined by the intersection of savings and investment schedules. The horizontal *II* line shows that investment is constant at the indicated level. *E* marks the spot where investment and savings curves intersect. Equilibrium GNP comes at the intersection of the *SS* and *II* curves because this is the only level of GNP at which the desired saving of households exactly matches the desired investment of business.

The figure shows that as the GNP (GDP) increases, so does the saving along SS. Further, investment II is autonomous and depends upon the business sentiment. Equilibrium GNP is determined at the intersection of saving and investment, or where the desired saving equals desired investment. Note that the GNP at M is much below where full employment is possible. In order to achieve full employment, either investment should rise to intersect saving at Q^PQ^P or saving should fall to intersect investment at Q^PQ^P, or both should shift to intersect at full employment. This figure can also demonstrate the paradox of thrift. So, if the saving curve moves north, investment remaining where it is, it leads to a fall in aggregate income, and thus a further fall in saving assuming the propensity to save is unchanged. This idea challenges Smith's dictum that appeared in his *The Theory of Moral Sentiments*: 'What is prudence in the conduct of every private family, can scarce be folly in that of a great Kingdom.' Conversely, if consumption increases, aggregate income increases, which leads to a rise in saving.

It follows that if private investment is insufficient to ensure full employment, help from the state is required. Keynes, in fact, gave a role to the state to intervene so that free enterprise at the micro-level could prosper. Many Keynesian converts thus called him the saviour of capitalism. The Second World War finally vindicated the Keynesian theory. With burgeoning war expenditure and borrowing, unemployment was wiped out. 'The Age of Keynes' had commenced.

Representatives from forty-four countries met at Bretton Woods in 1944 to address the problems that had made Keynes famous in the first place: the errors of post-First World War reparations and Churchill's return to the gold standard. As Galbraith puts in his *The Age of Uncertainty*, 'It was a conference of nations with Keynes.' The International Bank for Reconstruction and Development—which went on to become part of what is now known as the World Bank—and the International Monetary Fund (IMF) came into existence. The former was to help in the rebuilding of the war-torn

nations keeping in mind the mistakes of the previous war; the
latter to provide elbow room for currencies, permitting nations to
buy time by borrowing from the IMF. The gold standard lost some
of its rigidity.

Keynes, a principal architect of the World Bank and the IMF, died
of a heart attack—his second—in 1946.

The Keynesians

Keynes's end did not mark the end of his ideas. His ideas continued to rule the industrial world for the next three decades. The prevention of unemployment became the stated goal of successive governments in the US and Britain with the result that the Keynesian prescription of borrowing and spending during a recession, and tightening money supply and raising taxes in boom conditions became the standard formula. Barring a few shallow recessions, the industrial nations witnessed unprecedented prosperity during the next three decades.

Of the many Keynesians who dominated the intellectual climate of the times, we shall talk briefly about three. Skousen talks about these in his *The Big Three in Economics*: Alvin A. Hansen (1887–1975) who was known as the American Keynes, John Kenneth Galbraith (1908–2006) who was called the high priest of Keynesian thought, and Paul Alvin Samuelson (1915–2009) whose famous textbook educated generations of young economists in the US and beyond in Keynesian economics.

Hansen who moved to Harvard in 1937 simplified Keynesian concepts, which we know were difficult to understand from reading his General Theory. His work *A Guide to Keynes* was published in 1953. Hansen lectured on the importance of fiscal policy and Samuelson was among his many students. What discredited Hansen, however, was his mature economy or Stagnation Thesis, which averred that as nations grew richer and the saving rate rose, a lack of innovation and investment would cause them to stagnate especially in the light of a declining population. Facts proved Hansen wrong. As Skousen writes in his *The Making of Modern Economics*, the rich nations prospered as never before.

Galbraith was literally the tallest economist at six feet eight inches. Of Scottish descent, Galbraith was born in Canada and earned his doctorate in agricultural economics from the University of California, Berkeley. He learnt Keynesian theory during the year he spent at Cambridge, England, and became an instant convert. Galbraith served as the US ambassador to India from 1961 to 1963. (It was during this period that the author had the privilege of meeting him and listening to his lectures.) It is hard to imagine an economist who put so much humour into his lectures and prose. His Harvard students could never have believed economics to be a dismal science.

Galbraith was at heart a philosopher who questioned the trickle-down effect of the capitalist system and like Veblen was concerned about the affluence of the rich contrasting with the living standards of the poor. He describes this in his famous work entitled *The Affluent Society* (1958). In his magnum opus *The New Industrial State* (1967), he talks about the nexus between the government and the growing military–industrial complex. In addition, he talks of a few big firms controlling the market and squeezing out competition, thereby reducing the need for innovation. This, he warns, will ultimately hurt society. Skousen alludes to how, since facts proved otherwise, *The New Industrial State* did not have the impact Galbraith had envisioned.

Samuelson was the first American economist to win the Nobel Memorial Prize in 1970. His magnum opus *Foundations of Economic Analysis* based on his doctoral dissertation at Harvard purported to derive 'a general theory of economic theories', that is, how operationally meaningful theories can be arrived at from a small number of analogous methods. In *Foundations of Economic Analysis*, it is proposed that two general hypothesis are sufficient for this purpose: (a) the maximizing behaviour of consumers as to utility and business firms as to profit and (b) the economic system inclusive of a market and an economy in stable equilibrium.

For our purpose, however, what made Samuelson famous was his *Economics*, first published in 1948 and now in its nineteenth edition. It is in this book that he explained Keynesian economics to students the world over. While Samuelson taught at the Massachusetts Institute of Technology (MIT), it would not be wrong to say that every economics department is familiar with this book.

'With such famous supporters of Keynes,' a student wants to know, 'what happened after thirty years?'

What happened was a 400 per cent increase in oil prices as a result of the Arab petroleum exporting countries banding together to teach the US a lesson for supporting Israel in the Yom Kippur War of 1973–4. As oil prices shot up, economic growth in the industrial world came to a grinding halt. Oil being a vital input, prices in general went up and so did unemployment. The economy stagnated and inflation rose. A new term was coined—'stagflation'.

This put the Keynesians in a quandary. Until now, they had relied on the Phillips Curve—so named after A.W. Phillips who demonstrated in his paper 'The Relation between Unemployment and the Rate of Change of Money Wage Rates in the United Kingdom, 1861–1957' (1958), based on British data, that there was trade-off between inflation and employment. What this meant was that greater inflation would be the price for lesser unemployment and vice versa. This relationship had broadly held prior to the oil shock. Now with inflation and stagnation (unemployment) moving in the same direction, a major assumption of Keynesian economics was in question.

Was the economy really demand-driven as proposed by Keynes or was it driven by supply (production) as proposed by Say? In the present case, the supply of oil, which affected the cost of production of practically all output, seemed to weigh in favour of Say.

Samuelson nevertheless disagreed with this argument. In his *Economics*, he says, 'Supply shocks produce higher prices, followed by a decline in output and an increase in unemployment. Supply shocks thus lead to a deterioration of all the major goals of macroeconomic policy.' Figure 1 explains this phenomenon in terms of the aggregate supply (AS) and the aggregate demand (AD) curve.

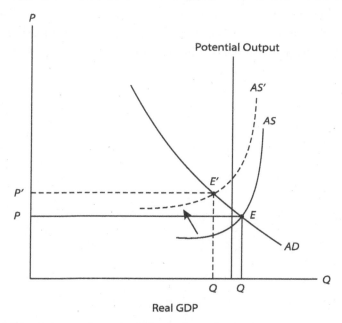

Figure 1 Effects of Supply Shocks

Source: Samuelson and Nordhaus (1992 [1948]).

Note: Sharply higher oil, commodity, or labour costs increase the cost of doing business. This leads to stagflation—stagnation combined with inflation. In the *AS–AD* framework, the higher costs shift the *AS* curve up from *AS* to *AS'* and the equilibrium shifts from *E* to *E'*. Output declines from *Q* to *Q'*, while prices rise. The economy thus suffers a double whammy—lower output and higher prices.

In other words, the oil shock was a case of the AS curve shifting backwards, thus explaining higher prices and lower employment—or stagflation.

According to Skousen's *The Making of Modern Economics*, Keynesians believed that Keynesian economics was robust and that stagflation was explainable.

The tide, however, was turning and the second oil shock of 1978 did not help the Keynesian cause. A quiet revolution that had been brewing for the past thirty years under the stewardship of Hayek was now coming to a head. We next talk of Hayek and his impact on macroeconomics.

The Duel Begins

Born in Vienna, Friedrich von Hayek was sixteen years younger than Keynes. A protégé of Mises, Hayek, like his mentor, predicted the Great Crash of 1929 during the mid-1920s. The British and American economists in the early 1930s were grappling with the reasons for this disaster and many looked towards the Austrian School for answers. Meanwhile, Robbins of the LSE visited Vienna and invited Hayek to deliver a series of lectures at the LSE.

Hayek brought with him three core beliefs from the Austrian School. First, that aggregates are misleading when talking about changing price levels since prices are set between individual buyers and sellers who have their own motives, and the choices made by individuals are diverse to the point where they defy measurement. Furthermore, as Hayek pointed in his paper 'On the Relationship between Investment and Output' (1934), it is futile 'to establish *direct* casual connections between the *total* quantity of money, the general level of all prices and, perhaps, also the *total* amount of production'.

Second, that trying to tame the business cycle through monetary measures like changing the interest rate or the extension or contraction of bank credit is counterproductive since it interferes with the natural process of reaching equilibrium. This observation relied on Wicksell's loanable funds theory that appeared in his *Interest and Prices*. Wicksell (1881–1926) makes a clear distinction between the 'natural' rate and 'market' rate of interest.

Wicksell defines the *natural* rate as that where the demand and supply of savings converge as shown by DD and SS in Figure 1. Savings in this sense are a function of the interest rate offered. Remember Keynes linked savings to income. The *market* rate, on the other hand, is that at which banks are willing to lend. So if banks lower the lending rate below the *natural* rate as shown by S¹S¹ in Figure 1, they will encourage boom conditions or an upswing of the business cycle. Thereafter, by pulling inflation back, they will actually push the economy towards a slump. Many believed they witnessed this phenomenon in the behaviour of the Federal Reserve before and after the crash of 1929. Therefore, ideally the *natural* rate and the *market* rate should be kept in sync— which, in effect, implies just waiting out a slump or a boom.

The third belief was based on Böhm-Bawerk, according to whom industrial production involves a degree of 'roundaboutness', a

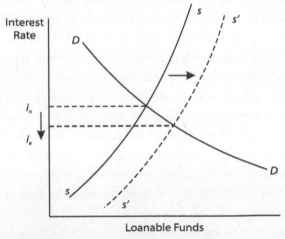

Figure 1

Source: Skousen (2001: 309).

point he puts across in his *The Positive Theory of Capital* (1891). This means that more capital-intensive methods of production, even as they are time-consuming to set up, would eventually result in greater efficiency and productivity. A simple example is the efficiency of catching fish by hand compared to catching them using a fishing net. Clearly, making a fishing net is time-consuming and costly, but it leads to a bigger catch—a good example of a roundabout method. Furthermore, in a slump, it should be easier to get rid of fish than to sell a fishing net. Extending this example to capital goods, selling the final product is simpler than it is to find buyers for plant and machinery, which Hayek believed was a reason for a long period of recovery after a recession.

Hayek extended this concept to his famed 'triangles', which he presented in his initial lecture upon arriving in England in 1931. The lecture was delivered to the Marshall Society at Cambridge before Austin Robinson, his wife Joan, Richard Kahn, Piero Sraffa, and James Meade, among others—or the 'Cambridge circus', as Nicholas Wapshott called them in his 'Keynes-Hayek: The Clash that Defined Modern Economics' (2011). Each triangle purported to convey that production starts with raw materials and proceeds through different stages of manufacture or value addition and ends at the point of retail. This was depicted by stage-wise progress from the narrow end of the triangle to its broad end. The shape of the triangle would change depending upon boom or bust conditions, as Hayek explained through his intricate diagrams. The 'Cambridge circus' thoroughly immersed in Keynesian economics could make neither head nor tail of Hayek's lecture.

Upon returning to London, a much disappointed Hayek was now given a special forum to hold forth to a specially invited audience. This was arranged by Robbins who had a double agenda—to bring Austrian economics to England and to defeat Keynesian notions on his home turf.

Hayek, who had suffered from a fever during his first lecture and had to compress the material prepared for four lecturers into one, was now welcomed by a much friendlier audience. His four lectures were a great success and a thoroughly impressed Robbins, whose goal was to counter the spreading influence of the Cambridge School, was only too pleased to bring to the LSE the great tradition of the Austrian School. William Beveridge offered Hayek a visiting professorship at the LSE, which was followed by the Tooke Chair in Economic Science and Statistics the next year.

Keynes meanwhile had just published his *Treatise on Money*, a labour of seven years. This became a fitting target for Hayek who pointed out its many logical flaws. Keynes, while admitting that he had moved on during the seven long years of writing this book, was not one to let go of a challenge. Though preoccupied with composing his *General Theory of Employment, Interest and Money*, Keynes did find the time to read Hayek's *Prices and Production* (1931). As documented by D.E. Moggridge in his *Maynard Keynes: An Economist's Biography* (1992), Keynes is said to have remarked the following about Hayek's work: 'The book as it stands, seems to me to be one of the most frightful muddles I have ever read—and yet it remains a book of some interest, which is likely to leave its mark on the mind of the reader.'

The duel between Keynes and Hayek continued in the pages of the LSE journal *Economica* as well as through private correspondence. Hayek just could not bring himself to accept that easing bank credit or using the monetary mechanism to come out of a slump was sensible, thus countering the idea that a little inflation was useful. It would be like what Professor Paul McCracken described in his class at Ann Arbor, that those who advocated a little pregnancy failed to realize that it would not remain 'little'. In fact, Hayek heralded the Monetarist School, which would unfold over the next few decades. In the meantime, Keynes, well before the publication of the *General Theory*, was advocating the importance of spending on the part of consumers and of borrowing and spending on the part of the government. The immediate problem, he said, was to get idle plant and machinery back into production and to give work to the vast number of the unemployed. As the Great Depression wore on without an end in sight, Hayek and the classical economists were unable to come up with a solution. Yet Hayek stuck to his guns.

'What really was the difference in the arguments of Keynes and Hayek?' *a student wants to know.*

By now we are familiar with Keynes's viewpoint, as it has been discussed in detail in an earlier chapter. Hayek's approach will require some elaboration.

Hayek had come away from Vienna in the years after the First World War where he had observed first-hand the ravages of inflation and the suffering it caused. Now in the 1930s, though ensconced with his wife Helen and their two children in the liberal confines of Britain, Hayek observed with growing alarm the steady rise to power of Hitler in Germany. The annexation of Austria by Germany finally prompted him to take British citizenship. It also sparked in him a visceral dislike of any form of centralized authority, which included both fascism and socialism. Added to this was the fact that he belonged to the classical-school tradition where the free market and democracy were inseparable.

The rise of the Soviet Union in these years as an economic power, albeit behind the iron curtain, had impressed many in Britain, including intellectuals like Joan Robinson and Beatrice Webb who were in thrall of Russia after having been given conducted tours to the accompaniment of the Stalinist propaganda. Stalin's blood-stained legacy remained hidden for the time being from the outside world. Many in England, and especially in Cambridge, had become converts to the socialist way of thinking, given the seemingly endless misery of the working classes.

Keynes, no socialist and one who abhorred any encroachment on personal liberty, was keen to find a way to revive the credibility of capitalism. His answer lay in his speeches to the lay public and the establishment prior to the General Theory and to the academia thereafter. In the US, he gave a push to Franklin D. Roosevelt's New Deal and at the same time converted many young economists flocking to Washington, DC, from leading American universities. In essence, what Keynes said was that spending on public works by borrowing would unleash the multiplier process and raise employment and investment. And once full employment was attained, there would be no need for further government spending and past deficits would be made up by surplus tax revenues. Further, easing money supply would be needed only in a slump and should not be used after full recovery.

Hayek's answer was that no amount of monetary easing had helped the US economy so far and it was a method that would have its adverse repercussion in the long run. To this, Keynes had famously remarked on an occasion, 'In the long run we are all dead.' Hayek was not in favour of monetary measures, which caused a divergence between the 'natural rate' and the 'market rate' of interest. According to him, adopting monetary measures, even by way of borrowing for public expenditure, would be like trying to tame the business cycle through methods that caused it in the first place. On the other hand, if loans were taken by the industry for further expansion and were given by the public from its savings, then planned saving and planned investment would be equal—a notion challenged by Keynes's concept of 'liquidity preference'.

While this debate proceeded, the public, the establishment, and the economics profession required immediate answers for the dire situation in which the free world found itself. Hayek had no answer. Keynes had the General Theory.

Mont Pèlerin

Asked many years later why he did not confront Keynes or point out the logical flaws in the General Theory, Hayek seemed evasive. Perhaps Hayek felt that Keynes's work was macroeconomic or top-down whereas economic behaviour, which involved a myriad individual choices, would only be understood through a bottom-up or microeconomic approach. In a sense, he was right because 'macroeconomics' was hardly known at that time. The fact remains that Hayek never came up with a cogent criticism of Keynes's General Theory. He instead busied himself in writing his *The Pure Theory of Capital* (1941), which he envisioned as his magnum opus and his answer to the General Theory. Riddled with many breaks, Hayek finally completed the work in 1940, and it was published the following year. However, as Hayek mentions in his *The Pure Theory of Capital*, even his great admirer Milton Friedman pronounced the book 'unreadable'.

It was not the best of times for Hayek. Some of his brightest pupils like Nicholas Kaldor and John Hicks had joined the Keynesian bandwagon.

Furthermore, once the war began and London became a target for Hitler's bombers, the LSE was shifted to Cambridge. Hayek now shared wartime duties with Keynes. During this period, both avoided discussing economics with each other and shared a warm relationship.

In 1944, *The Road to Serfdom*, Hayek's rather pessimistic but important work, was published in Britain. The University of Chicago Press soon picked it up in America and it became a bestseller much against Hayek's expectations. Keynes was among those who read it soon after its publication, and he was all praise for it. As Skousen cites in his *The Making of Modern Economics*, Keynes said, '... morally and philosophically I find myself in complete agreement with virtually the whole of it; and not only in agreement with it, but in a deeply moved agreement.' He, however, went on to point out that planning in the hands of those who share your moral values can be a good thing, but in the hands of those who do not, it can be dangerous. Keynes left Hayek with the riddle as to where to draw the line between too much planning and too little of it. While Hayek could not answer this directly, he did hold on to his belief that only if the private sector in a competitive economy could not do the job should the government step in; for instance, in organizing a comprehensive social insurance system.

Academics generally felt that Hayek had overstated his case against any form of government intervention in the economy. Winston Churchill, on the other hand, picked up many ideas from *The Road to Serfdom* for his address to the nation in 1945. The sales of this book soared while at the same time dividing 'the Left from the Right and the Right from the ultra-right'. Hayek experienced both abuse and praise in America, depending on which side of the divide the reader stood.

The Road to Serfdom was not a tract on economic theory. Rather, it was a voice of caution against authoritarian regimes—the likes of which Hayek observed in Hitler's fascist Germany and Stalin's communist Russia. His fear was that even elected governments in democracies could go too far in the direction of economic planning, thus interfering with the free market mechanism. The book, however, fell flat among the academics—and in spite of the encouraging sales of the book, Hayek felt he had discredited himself among his fellow economists.

Hayek noticed another thing in America. Keynesianism was so widespread that even ordinary people felt socialism was not only inevitable but also good. Those who agreed with Hayek felt isolated. They believed a free market alternative was needed against Keynesian ideas. It gradually dawned on Hayek that he could become the voice of an anti-Keynesian movement. Towards this end, he sought to bring together like-minded people at a common forum. This eventually took the shape of a ten-day conference in 1947. The venue was Hotel du Parc located virtually on the summit of Mont Pèlerin, which overlooked Lake Geneva in Switzerland. Some rich bankers and foundations who believed in the cause of liberal economics funded the event.

Among those who attended were Mises, Fritz Machlup, Robbins, Frank Knight, George Stigler, and Karl Popper. Most importantly, it was attended by a young man, barely thirty-five years old, from Chicago. His name was Milton Friedman. A Keynesian at that point, Friedman was to carry the mantle of the Monetarist School in later years. This conference and the subsequent ones were intensely stormy at times. Hayek nevertheless believed they would carry the liberal movement forward.

In the meantime, there was a storm brewing in Hayek's personal life. He was contemplating a divorce from Helen, his wife of twenty years. He intended to marry his childhood sweetheart and cousin Helene. He eventually did by joining the University of Arkansas in Fayetteville where marriage laws were more permissive, and obtained a divorce. This personal move did not go down well with his close friend Robbins and other members of the economics faculty at the LSE, who refused to speak to Hayek.

'How could such a serious-minded man be so irresponsible?' A student seems surprised—perhaps even a tad offended.

Matters of the heart are always unpredictable; they know no reason.

In 1950, Hayek moved to the US and in time got a teaching post at the University of Chicago. While there, he wrote *The Constitution of Liberty* (1960), for which he garnered much praise. Shortly thereafter, Hayek moved to Germany, where he felt at home and taught at the University of Freiberg. Nonetheless, he suffered from ill health and occasional bouts of depression. This was to change when in 1974 he was told that he had been awarded the Nobel Prize in economics for his work on monetary theory and the business cycle. His mood lifted, despite the fact that he had to share the prize with Gunnar Myrdal who was a socialist and on the other side of the ideological divide. You may recall that Myrdal was the first to call India a soft state.

Hayek's health improved and he would go on to live until the age of ninety-two. The year 1974 was a significant year for him also for another reason. The oil crisis had hit the world and soon thereafter began the decline of Keynesian influence. Hayek could now claim that he had always believed Keynes's theories were flawed. In the 1980s, redemption came to Hayek in yet another form. Margaret Thatcher in England and Ronald Reagan in America both professed a liberal philosophy and their countries prospered. The prosperity during Reagan's presidency, however, came about—so the Keynesians claim—by the application of Keynesian medicine, which Reagan least understood. Thatcher, on the other hand, regarded *The Road to Serfdom* her economic bible and asked Hayek to tutor her during his periodic visits to England.

For those with a mind for symmetry, the first thirty years after the Second World War belonged to Keynes. Hayek and his followers claimed the next thirty years, beginning from 1978, the year of the second oil shock.

❧

The year of reckoning, however, was to come in 2008 when the world suffered another great recession.

The Great Monetarist

Milton Friedman (1912–2006) was born in a Jewish family in Brooklyn. Barely over five feet tall and coming from a frugal financial background, Friedman won a scholarship to Rutgers University and thereafter went on to study economics at the University of Chicago. It was here that he met his future wife Rose, who was the sister of Aaron Director, a member of the economics faculty. Among the other faculty members were great names like Frank Knight, Jacob Viner, and Henry Simons who surprisingly during the Great Depression advocated policies similar to those recommended by Keynes, namely fiscal deficits in bad times and pulling back when recovery was under way. In other words, they recognized the impotence of monetary policy during the times of depression and the need to rely on fiscal methods. Friedman himself believed in this.

During the war years, Friedman worked for the Treasury Department in Washington, DC, and later, after earning his PhD at Columbia University in 1946, went on to teach at the University of Chicago. Chicago, he declared, was 'my kind of town', where he devoted his time to teaching and research on issues related to money. His seminal work *A Monetary History of the United States, 1867–1960* (2008), co-authored with Anna Schwartz, examined every twist and turn of the business cycle during this period of nearly a century.

Friedman and Schwartz, after studying a voluminous amount of data about the years of the Great Depression, that is, 1929 to 1933, concluded that a shortage of money supply inadvertently engineered by the Federal Reserve after the crash of 1929 was the real culprit rather than, as Keynes had argued, an absence of aggregate demand. The data supported this explanation. Friedman believed that another cause of the problem was that the Federal Reserve did not publish money supply data. If it had, corrective steps would have been advised and the Depression would not have lasted so long. Money supply data, however, was published only after Friedman and Schwartz had invented the concepts of M1 (cash and checking accounts) and M2 (currency market deposits plus M1).

Friedman, an admirer of Fisher, was also able to point out the error he had made in placing the emphasis on the wrong variable in his formula $M \times V = P \times Q$. It was not the stability of price P, as Fisher believed, that mattered in predicting the business cycle. Rather it was the change in M or quantity of money. Friedman also explained the Phillips Curve, which he said brought about a temporary trade-off between unemployment and inflation. In the long run, inflation would lead to higher unemployment.

Despite these observations, the Keynesian influence prevailed until well into the 1970s, when the world faced the oil shocks. Interestingly, it was also around this time (1976) that Friedman got the Nobel Prize.

'Was Friedman's thinking in line with Hayek's or was there a difference?' a student wants to know.

Hayek belonged to the Austrian School, which focused on the stages of production even though he and Mises had recognized an oversupply of money prior to 1929 as a factor contributing to the Great Depression. Nevertheless, Hayek believed that the money supply should be kept in tight control and the business cycle should be allowed to play itself out. Friedman, who belonged to the Chicago School, placed great emphasis on monetary policy in regulating the economy.

Hayek and Friedman, however, shared their belief in the importance of the neoclassical school, which advocated free competition, an absence of monopolies, and minimal interference of the government in the affairs of the economy. This led to the argument for and against large governments and took on political overtones in the decades after the 1970s.

In consequence, the economics profession was divided between the so-called 'salt water' and 'fresh water' economists. The former of the Keynesian bent of mind belonged to universities on the eastern and western sea boards of the US, whereas the latter to the Midwestern universities in the neighbourhood of Lake Michigan, notably the University of Chicago.

The story, however, does not end here. The Great Recession that struck the US in 2008 and thereafter spread to the rest of the world deserves an explanation. It took the form of a banking crisis to which Keynesian remedies were applied. Who was to blame: the Keynesians or the Monetarists?

We shall return to this later, after we have examined the ideas of some other post-Keynesian economists.

'Why do you want to break the link?'

There is no broken link here. The aim is to bring into the mainstream economists who can enlighten us on a different set of problems. Those we have covered so far speak about the concerns and issues related to the developed economies, which account for just about 20 per cent of the world's population. The rest live in the poor countries of Asia, Africa, and Latin America and share problems of a very different nature from those of the industrial world.

The Development Economist

The term 'post-Keynesian' generally refers to the decades after the oil shocks of the 1970s, when the Keynesian influence began to wane. We, however, can also define it as the era that began after Keynes's death soon after the war ended. This was the time when a number of Asian, African, and Latin American countries were winning independence from colonial rule and had to cope with a legacy of economic backwardness and poverty.

It was in these years that economists began to focus on the problems of economic development in what were then called the 'backward economies'. Many famous names contributed to growth economics such as Roy Harrod, Robert Lucas, and Robert Solow, among others. We, however, shall focus on only three: William Arthur Lewis (1915–1991), Bhagwati, and Sen. Of these, the first was of African descent and the latter two are of Indian descent. Lewis wrote extensively on growth models applicable to the developing countries, Bhagwati on international trade models with reference to the world as a whole as well as to the developing economies, and Sen has covered a number of subsets of economics with a special focus on welfare, ethics, and justice.

Lewis was born in Saint Lucia in the Caribbean. He completed school at the age of fourteen, earned his B.Sc. degree in 1937 and PhD from the LSE in 1940. In 1947, Lewis married Gladys Jacobs. In the same year, he was selected to teach at the University of Manchester in the UK. It was here that he became interested in development economics with reference to the countries that had begun to gain independence from their colonial masters.

Lewis's seminal work titled 'Economic Development with Unlimited Supplies of Labour' was published in *The Manchester School* in 1954. The voluminous *The Theory of Economic Growth* followed the next year. Lewis was the first person of African origin to win the Nobel Prize for economics in 1979. We shall rely here on his 1954 paper, wherein he discusses both a 'closed economy' and an 'open economy'.

According to Lewis, Keynesian economics, while dealing with mass unemployment or surplus labour during a cyclical recession, considered the problem solved once capital in the form of machines was again fully employed since there should then be no unemployment. This model was clearly not suited to underdeveloped countries like Egypt, India, or Jamaica, which suffered from an ongoing superfluity of labour. The neoclassical model was also not applicable since by the 1870s labour shortages were on the horizon and the notion of the *iron law of wages* was in retreat. Having set aside both these models, Lewis looked to the classical framework, first in a closed and then in an open economy.

Speaking of a closed economy, Lewis defines an unlimited supply of labour in the context where the population is so large in relation to capital and other natural resources that its marginal productivity is close to zero. As R. Nurkse explains in his 'Notes on Unbalanced Growth' (1959), labour here takes on various forms such as 'disguised' unemployment, which is rampant on farms that support a large number of family members. The migration of some members to other avenues of employment in such cases does not adversely affect the farm output. Another example of surplus labour is seen in the casual job sector where young men at railway stations run to pick up your bags or a large number of retail shop owners end up making a small income whereas bulk retailing requiring capital would raise the total revenue and employment. Unfortunately, such alternative avenues of employment are not available to them.

Lewis then goes on to describe the plethora of domestic servants employed by the rich, the messengers who sit yawning outside offices or those who hang out around courtyards. It would almost seem as if he is talking about India, though, in fact, he is covering a much larger canvas of countries. It turns out that even where people are working for wages, their marginal productivity is negligible. For the period Lewis was describing, the pattern of women working outside their home was not uniform even in Britain. He, therefore, spelt out the immense opportunities that would be available with the use of a little capital and organization in teaching children, knitting, stitching, and so on. In India, women to this day contribute significantly in the construction industry and other low capital using occupations like fetching water and farming.

To this pool of available labour, Lewis adds the increase in population as a result of more births than deaths. At this point, he brings in Ricardo and Malthus. Both Ricardo and Malthus believed that an increase in population is caused by economic development. They did not, however, separately analyse the effect of the death rate. Lewis separates the impact of the birth rate from the death rate, but strongly believes that population increase is of interest only if it can be shown to be positively related to economic development.

As for the birth rate, there is no evidence to prove that it has a directly proportional relationship with economic development. In fact, in the West the birth rate declined during the high growth years of the later part of the nineteenth and in the twentieth centuries. In that sense it runs counter to the belief in the *iron law* of *wages* that the classical economists held to be true, namely that a greater availability of food leads to higher birth rates. Lewis, however, argues that the growth of population is demonstrably related to the decline in death rate, which results from the discovery of new drugs, their availability worldwide, and better medical facilities. In consequence, the supply of labour in the developing countries is quite inexhaustible.

There is a twist in the argument here based on Marx's propagation of Ricardo's idea that machinery displaces labour. Not only that, but also that large-scale industry swallows small businesses and the petty bourgeoisie, thus leading to the creation of an industrial reserve army. Lewis chooses to ignore this argument. He moves on instead to the bottlenecks created by the absence of trained workers like masons, electricians, welders, engineers, and administrators. These shortages he deems as temporary and possible to overcome. The real bottleneck, he believes, is the absence of capital and natural resources and once these are available, the development of skills follows, albeit with a time lag.

The secret therefore lies in the development of a capitalized sector, which can draw workers from subsistence occupations, thereby raising the output per head. Further, the capitalist sector need not be monolithic. It can grow in competing as well as complementary areas.

The floor to the wages is set by the subsistence sector but in the capitalized sector they will be significantly higher on account of having to attract people from an easygoing lifestyle and because the cost of living in urbanized industrial centres is invariably higher. Nevertheless, the capitalist sector earns a surplus, which if reinvested leads to further surplus. Capital accumulation thus takes place in stages by bringing into employment more and more people from the subsistence sector until in theory at least, no more subsistence labour is left. Figure 1 depicts this.

In the figure, OS is what subsistence worker earns, OW the wage in the capitalist sector, and WN_1Q_1 the surplus in the initial stage.

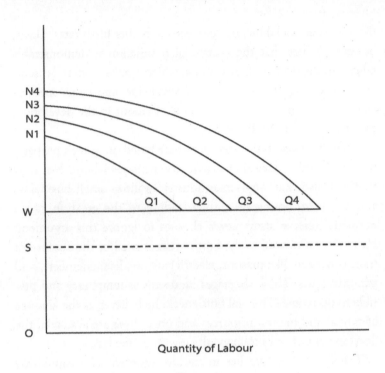

Figure 1

Source: Lewis (1954: 8).

As part of this surplus is reinvested, the fixed capital increases and the marginal productivity curve of labour moves to $N_2 Q_2$. Both surplus and employment rise by stages, as more capital is invested until $N_4 Q_4$ is reached.

There is the further question of whether technical knowledge needs to be distinguished from capital investment. Lewis feels it is not necessary as both go towards enhancing output.

Lewis then proceeds to discuss how the classical economists would have viewed the capitalist surplus. Malthus was worried about a glut of commodities that would result from surplus output. Ricardo disagreed. He believed that what the capitalists did not consume would go into the payment of wages for the creation of more capital, thus making possible a new round of employment. Then came Malthus's final argument that if savings are indeed used for investment and there is no hoarding, the rate of profit on capital must surely fall since capital investment is growing faster than consumption and eventually there will come a time when it is not worth investing more. Ricardo thought this was impossible since the supply of labour is unlimited, which is true under the classical model where the capital-to-labour ratio can be held constant and so also the rate of profit on capital. It was only under the neoclassical model that capital was shown to grow faster than the labour supply.

The one worry that Ricardo had was that land prices or rent to the landowners would rise with greater capital investment, thus transferring the benefits of capital surpluses to the landowner. This, as we know, has not come about in practice, especially because with the rising productivity on land (much against the predictions of Malthus), the benefits of the lower prices of food accrue to the workers and finally to the capitalist sector. The capitalist sector also benefits from technical progress.

Another issue of crucial importance to economic development that Lewis raises is of the growth of voluntary saving. In fact, as R.K. Kanth cites in his *Paradigms in Economic Development: Classic Perspectives, Critiques, and Reflections* (1994), Lewis goes so far as to say that 'we cannot explain any "industrial" revolution (as the economic historians pretend to do) until we can explain why saving increased relatively to national income'. He contends that in developing countries with surplus labour, about 10 per cent of those with the largest incomes receive close to 40 per cent of the national income (as was probably true for India after Independence) and, therefore, are in the best position to save. Per contra, the remaining 90 per cent have hardly any scope to save. Here Lewis brings in a civilizational argument about the rise of savings. Where there is technological advancement, the scope and returns from capital investment are high. On the other hand, if a civilization is technologically stagnant, the tendency will be to invest more in buildings and monuments. This was seen to be the case in England after and prior to the Industrial Revolution.

As Kanth cites in his work, Lewis's argument finally turns on the point 'that saving increases relatively to national income because the incomes of the savers increase relatively to the national income'. Further, 'practically all the saving is done by people who receive profits or rents'. Understandably, the distribution of incomes is skewed in favour of the saving classes.

Lewis then refutes the point that capital accumulation in Britain was made possible by the spate of inventions that came about during the Industrial Revolution. It does not gel with the neoclassical theory in the sense that not only did the marginal productivity of capital go up but also that of labour since by that time labour was becoming scarce. This is also in sync with neoclassical assumption that capital accumulation could not be attributed to the marginal productivity of capital alone. However, according to Lewis, 'it fits beautifully into the modified classical model, since in this model practically the whole benefit of inventions goes into the surplus, and becomes available for further capital accumulation.'

'This is not clear,' says a student. 'What is the modified classical model?'

Let us go back and start with the Keynesian model that Lewis rejects. According to Lewis, the Keynesian model addresses the problems caused by the business cycle during a depression when labour is unemployed despite the existence of unutilized machines and facilities. Once the cycle moves up with help from the state, unemployment disappears. However, this is unlike the problem faced by developing countries with unlimited supplies of labour.

The neoclassical model, on the other hand, addresses the problem of achieving equilibrium with the optimal allocation of all factors of production that are in limited supply. Labour, in this case, has an upward-sloping supply curve similar to that for land or capital and, therefore, capital accumulation cannot be attributed to any one factor. The Keynesian model thus does not apply to a case of unlimited supply of labour.

The classical model could still be applied with some modification. It holds that the supply of labour is unlimited based on the iron law of wages, that is, if the food supply increases, the birth rate will rise ensuring a continuous supply of labour. Lewis modifies this model by relying on a decline in the death rate through better medication, to ensure an unlimited supply of labour in relation to a limited supply of capital—a fact in the case of developing economies.

Let us give Lewis's model a reality check with reference to India. It does turn out that the birth rate (per 1,000) dropped steadily from forty-nine in the decade of 1901–11 to forty-two in 1951–61 and further to twenty in 2001–11. For the same decades, the death rates (per 1,000) declined rather steeply: forty-three, twenty-three, and seven-and-a-half. So far, this is in line with Lewis's prediction. What he does not factor in, however, is the rise in the life expectancy. For the same decades, it went up from twenty-three to forty-one to seventy years, as per various issues of SRS bulletins issued by the office of the Registrar General of India. The trends in any event point towards an abundant labour supply.

Lewis then goes on to argue that the inequality of incomes is not a sufficient condition for the increase in savings. In the poor and overpopulated countries, for example, the inequality of incomes is high and the landlords are the greatest beneficiaries. However, instead of investing in capital formation, landlords are prone to spending their rent income on consumption. Capitalists, on the other hand, are inclined to invest in capital formation. Therefore, if the income distribution favours the capitalist rather than the rent earner, capital formation will tend to be higher.

But what causes the growth of a capitalist class, especially in a society where the population is large and agriculture is the primary activity? In the early stages of development, most countries import their entrepreneurs from abroad, as happened in India during the nineteenth century. After Independence though, India found that there now existed a nascent but dynamic Indian business class.

Nehru put emphasis on developing state-owned enterprises, much like what had happened in the Soviet Union. Capital formation thus took place from ploughing back profits into the business of course, but also from taxing the rich and the middle class. Along with this, much hand labour (circulating capital) was used for building roads, canals, and other infrastructure without resorting to the use of heavy machinery or fixed capital. Indeed if hand labour with the simplest of tools can be used to create capital like in irrigation and construction, it will not lead to much diversion from consumption to investment. At the same time, it will be a great source for generating employment. Further, as Kanth cites in *Paradigms in Economic Development*, Lewis felt that as 'the opportunities for using capital productively increase rapidly, the surplus will grow rapidly, and the capitalist class with it.'

'Was Nehru a socialist?' asks a student.

Nehru was a Fabian socialist. What this means is that he was against a revolutionary or violent form of conversion to socialism, like that which had taken place in Soviet Russia. He instead favoured a reasoned approach to socialism, which he felt was best suited to a developing country like India. At the same time, Nehru was an admirer of the Soviet Gosplan, a system of five-year plans, which he adopted for India's economic development.

So far, the role of money in terms of bank credit has not been touched upon. According to the neoclassical model, all capital investment is generated by withdrawing resources from the manufacture of consumption goods and investing in capital formation. This is not the case in Lewis's model, as labour is plentiful and its marginal productivity zero. Further, in the real world, money supply plays a vital role because apart from profit, credit also helps in creating capital. However, as Lewis mentioned in his 'Economic Development with Unlimited Supplies of Labour': 'The difference between profit-financed and credit-financed capital is not in the ultimate effects on output, but in the immediate effects on prices and the distribution of incomes.' In other words, if new money is used for capital formation and not for producing consumer goods beyond their current level, the following will happen: the newly employed labour will spend on consumer goods, thus bidding up their prices. This will result in inflation, but only so long as the newly created capital takes to produce more consumer goods. What this means is that inflation will last only as long as profits increase to the extent that the next round of investment can be financed entirely out of profits without recourse to further borrowing. Lewis further clarifies, 'Inflation for purposes of capital formation is self destructive. Prices begin to rise, but are sooner or later overtaken by rising output, and may in the last state, end up lower than they were at the beginning.' In the interim, there is, of course, a redistribution of income, but as savings grow and catch up with investment, the economy arrives at a new equilibrium. Moreover, it is only in those countries where the industrial class is large or growing that inflation will lead to greater capital formation. In a telling statement, Lewis says, '[W]e should also note that many governments do not like the fact that inflation enables industrialists to earn the extra profits with which they create fixed capital, since this results in an increase of private fortunes.'

A word now on the role of governments: after the Second World War, governments in the industrial nations could tax up to 50 per cent of the marginal incomes; in the developing countries, they could tax only a small percentage. '[O]ne of the worst off is India,' Lewis said in the context of the 1950s, 'with a large part of its output produced by subsistence producers and small scale units, hard to reach, and with less than 10 per cent of national income passing in foreign trade.'

'Was this really true?'

This observation appears odd as I clearly recall that in these years India had a thriving textile industry, a growing sugar industry, a large steel mill, and a modern sewing machine factory, all in the private sector.

The next important line of thought developed by Lewis concerns the terms of trade between industry and agriculture. In order for capital accumulation to take place, the productivity of industry and agriculture must both grow. If, for example, agriculture produces only food and industry products unrelated to food and if agriculture is stagnant, capital accumulation will eventually come to a halt. On the other hand, if agricultural productivity grows faster than that of industry, the subsistence wage will rise and the terms of trade will hit industry adversely because of a rise in industrial wages. This happened in the Soviet Union when farm productivity rose and subsistence wages went up. The state then intervened to raise the prices of manufactures and taxed the collective farms so that capital formation could progress faster. In the final analysis, however, if capital accumulation proceeds faster than the growth of population, there should come a time when there is no labour surplus and wages in all sectors rise. Smith had foreseen this.

'How far are we in India from a time when there will be no labour surplus?'

An excellent question, indeed. Let us look at the rate of capital formation and the actual figures of employment.

The saving rate, which we shall treat as the same as the rate of capital formation, grew from 9 per cent to 12 per cent during the decade from 1951 to 1961. By 1991, it was 23 per cent, 25 per cent by 2000, and 34 per cent by 2011. This reflects a long-term trend in the growth of capital formation. The question now is how far are we from achieving full employment.

According to the National Sample Survey Office round 2011–12, the total number of men and women in the employable age group are 480 million (with some rounding off). Of these, just under 30 million are employed in organized industry in both private and public sectors. They produce goods for direct consumption as well as intermediate goods and can therefore be defined as involved in direct capital formation. Then there are pure agricultural workers who constitute 245 million as per the 2009–10 census. That leaves around 205 million who could be called casual wage labourers engaged in farm or non-farm activities in public works such as road construction, building dams, flood relief, and so on. Much of the non-farm activity could be described as capital formation through 'hand labour'. As daily-wage earners, they are unlikely to be employed for the whole year. They, along with those in 'disguised employment' on the farms, form a huge pool of available labour earning close to subsistence wages. Capital formation in India thus has a long way to go before the entire supply of labour is exhausted.

We now come to the subject of the open economy. Once the labour supply is fully utilized in a closed economy, wages will begin to rise and the rate of growth of the capital surplus will decline. The capitalist will then begin to seek surplus workers at subsistence wages in other countries and bring them in through the immigration route. Else, he will export capital to the labour-surplus countries. The latter is generally an easier option, as labour unions are largely resistant to the import of foreign labour. A labour-surplus importing country views the export of capital favourably since it creates more employment. The US has imported labour from Puerto Rico and Mexico but the numbers are so small in relation to the US labour strength that they have not had any adverse impact on the wages of US workers.

However, the export of capital inclusive of technical knowledge is seen to bring much better returns from countries that not only have surplus labour available but also a rich infrastructure based on past capital investments. Take the example of the increasing number of foreign automobile companies that have come into India since the early 1990s largely because of the infrastructure that has come up. Further, if a country has abundant natural resources like oil, gas, or coal, it becomes a preferred destination for foreign direct investment. On the question of a declining rate of return on capital investment, Lewis presents Marshall's argument, which goes as follows: increasing capital investment per head tends to lower its yield, whereas if it is accompanied by increasing technical knowledge it tends to increase it. Therefore, we cannot prejudge whether the return on capital will rise or fall. That it will necessarily fall is 'a popular myth'. Also, if the rate of return in a particular line of business slows down, say, because of a saturation in the home market, the capitalist always has the option to invest abroad. On the other hand, the capitalist may choose to diversify into other lines of business.

Depending on the cost structure abroad, there could be better opportunities for returns on investment there even before the labour supply in the home market is exhausted. The one factor not mentioned by Lewis is the relative foreign exchange rate. If, for example, the currency of a foreign country is undervalued, the cost structure there will be favourable for the export of capital. This has been the case with the Chinese yuan in relation to the US dollar. Consequently, a huge amount of foreign direct investment has flowed into China. In varying degrees, this has also been the case with other developing countries. This implies that foreign direct investment has helped towards the further utilization of surplus labour. A similar argument applies in the case of differing interest rates between countries. A high interest rate in India, for example, in comparison to a low interest rate in the US accounts for a flow of foreign institutional investment to the former.

Lewis concludes by saying: 'The Law of Comparative Costs is just as valid in countries with surplus labour as it is in others. But whereas in the latter it is a valid foundation of arguments for free trade, in the former it is an equally valid foundation of arguments for protection.'

The Guru of International Trade

It was in 1966 at Harvard that I heard a buzz in the faculty about a young Indian who had written a brilliant article titled 'The Pure Theory of International Trade'. I was curious to find out more, and I found that he was someone I had met earlier in Delhi. The person was none other than the economist Jagdish Bhagwati, who was at that time teaching in the Delhi School of Economics. In the years to come, we became good friends.

The article that launched Bhagwati on the path to fame and global recognition is for us a good point to begin exploring some of his ideas. But before that, a bit about his early life. Born in 1934 into a Gujarati family, Bhagwati studied at Sydenham College in Mumbai and later completed his BA in economics from Cambridge University in the UK in 1956. His contemporaries there were none other than Sen and India's future prime minister Manmohan Singh. In 1967, Bhagwati received his PhD in economics from the MIT. He is married to Padma Desai, a specialist on Russia, and both teach at Columbia University.

Bhagwati has a number of awards to his credit and he has been a long-time contender for the Nobel Prize. His standing as an economist is best summed up in the words of Samuelson, who at the seventieth birthday festschrift conference in Gainesville Florida in January 2005, said:

I measure a scholar's prolific-ness not by the mere number of his publishings. Just as the area of a rectangle equals its width times its depth, the quality of a lifetime accomplishment must weigh each article by its novelties and wisdoms ... Jagdish Bhagwati is more like Haydn: a composer of more than a hundred symphonies and no one of them other than top notch.... In the struggle to improve the lot of mankind, whether located in advanced economies or in societies climbing the ladder out of poverty, Jagdish Bhagwati has been a tireless partisan of that globalization which elevates global total-factor–productivities both of richest America and poorest regions of Asia and Africa.

It will not be easy to take you through Bhagwati's 1964 article as it is highly technical and runs into eighty-four pages. Nevertheless, I will try to give you a cursory idea based on Ricardo, whom we have already discussed, and others like Eli Heckscher (1879–1952) and Bertil Ohlin (1899–1979).

Bhagwati divides the issues of pure trade theory into two categories. The first is the 'positive' or 'objective' analysis, which deals with questions like the composition of trade, how tariffs affect factor prices, and how trade affects the terms of trade. The second deals with 'welfare' or 'normative' questions like whether free trade maximizes world real income or would tariffs be better than subsidies as a form of government intervention.

Positive theory in turn looks at (a) 'static' equilibrium at any given point of time; (b) 'comparative statics', which compares equilibrium values at different points in time; and (c) 'dynamics', which traces the path between two different points in time. Finally, there is what Bhagwati calls the 'central limitation of trade theory' in terms of dealing with capital goods and intermediates that are essential for trade with developing countries.

'Was this last point discussed in your chapter on "The Trajectory of Partial Equilibrium Analysis"?' asks a student.

In a micro sense you could say that instead of 'intermediates' being an abstract concept, each intermediate in the form of a component goes into a consumer good or capital good. Given its own demand and production functions, it forms an integral part of domestic and/or international trade.

Then there are propositions on the welfare aspects such as 'free trade is better than no trade' as well as the cost–benefit analysis of different policy options. Central planners like in India have tried to incorporate certain welfare aspects of trade in their planning techniques.

With this brief overview we shall relook at the Ricardian theory of trade. As was demonstrated in a previous chapter using Ricardo's Portugal–England example, trade in welfare terms is beneficial for both trading partners. However, further research alluded to by Bhagwati also shows that Ricardo's concerns included both the normative and positive aspects of trade. Let us examine Ricardo's model in some detail. It assumes that between the two countries in question there are two commodities (cloth and wine), a single factor of production (labour), and constant returns to scale for both commodities. It follows that the pre-trade commodity price ratios will correspond to the output factor ratios in the production functions.

What this means is that the number of labour hours that went into the production of wine and cloth in England and Portugal, in relation to their respective prices prior to trade, remain the same after trade.

Therefore, for a closed economy with constant returns to scale for a single factor (labour), neither demand nor factor supply will impact the equilibrium commodity price ratio. Since Ricardo assumes similar domestic conditions for each trading partner, the composition of trade will be determined entirely by the 'international differences in the relative output-factor

If a_1 and a_2 are the output-factor ratios for country I and b_1 and b_2 for country II in activities 1 and 2 respectively, country I will export commodity 1 and import commodity 2 if $a_1 / a_2 > b_1/b_2$ (as this will imply that commodity 1 will be cheaper, and commodity 2 dearer, in country I than in country II prior to trade). The algebraic condition is frequently written as $a_1 / b_1 > a_2/b_2$, which states the condition in terms of 'comparative factor productivities'.

The Ricardian proposition, however, is strong only so long as we are dealing with two countries and two products. Once we extend it to two countries and many products, it is weakened. 'The precise composition of exports and imports,' according to Bhagwati, 'can be determined only by bringing demand into the model.' This is to say prices vary with volume.

A number of trade economists have empirically tested the two-country, multiple-product model with encouraging results. The quest, however, continues until we come to an alternate theory—that of Heckscher and Ohlin.

Heckscher and Ohlin, both Swedish economists, were teacher and student at the Stockholm School of Economics until Ohlin succeeded Heckscher as the professor of economics in 1930. Soon thereafter in 1933 Ohlin published his work on inter-regional and international trade based on an earlier work by Heckscher and his own research, which became famous as the Heckscher–Ohlin model. Ohlin was awarded the Nobel Prize in 1977.

The Heckscher–Ohlin model makes a departure from the Ricardian model in terms of the following assumptions. Ricardo assumes a single factor of production (labour) as well as constant returns to scale, thus making factor supply irrelevant in the determination of the trade pattern. Heckscher and Ohlin, on the other hand, postulate that a country's exports are driven by the intensive use of that factor in which it is abundant. This immediately assumes that there are at least two factors rather than one as in the case of the Ricardian model. It further assumes that the major factors, labour and capital, are not available in the same proportion between the two trading partners; the labour-to-capital ratio of the two goods traded differ; labour or capital are neither exported nor imported; there are no transportation costs; and the needs of the two trading partners are the same. These conditions, though restrictive, are still a significant relaxation of the Ricardian conditions since we are now talking about two trading partners, two factors, and multiple products. The theory depends on the ratio of capital to labour rather than their absolute amounts. This makes it possible for countries to specialize by using more of the factor that is abundant, whether it is labour or capital. Hence trade is possible between the developing and industrialized countries since the former can gain an advantage in exports by using more labour, which is abundant in relation to capital. The reverse should also be true for those countries that have an abundance of capital.

Further research by Samuelson and Nordhaus (published as *Economics*) showed that under certain conditions given perfect competition and profit maximization in perfect markets, the relationship between factor and commodity price ratios will be unique. This means that each product will have one, and only one, factor-to-price ratio at equilibrium. In consequence, capital-intensive production will be cheaper in countries that are abundant in capital. Similarly, labour-intensive production will be cheaper in countries where labour is plentiful.

The Heckscher–Ohlin hypothesis was actually empirically tested by W. Leontief by measuring the structure of American exports and imports in terms of their capital-to-labour ratio. His paper 'Mathematics in Economics' was published in 1954. The result was rather startling and is known as the Leontief paradox. America's exports were labour-intensive and its imports capital-intensive. There have been many attempts towards rescuing the

Heckscher–Ohlin hypothesis from this apparent contradiction, some by Leontief himself.

Leontief's explanation turns to the definition of human capital. As he puts it, American labour was about three times as efficient in its export industries as in, say, agriculture and was paid much more than the national average. Therefore, the labour-to-capital ratio in value terms was higher and could explain the anomaly in the structure of exports and imports. This explanation was considered by many to be unsatisfactory as there was no empirical basis to suggest that American labour was thrice as efficient as in the importing country. Bhagwati, in fact, takes us through a number of studies by trade economists attempting to test empirically the Heckscher–Ohlin hypothesis in terms of trade between the US and Britain, the US and Canada, the US and Japan, and between the US and India. In short, Bhagwati believes that the Heckscher–Ohlin model can be adapted usefully if it is stated in terms of 'each pair of trading countries' rather than in 'aggregate terms'. Alternate theories are also discussed, which we shall skip as the two mentioned here continue to hold sway. In fact, so much has been added to the work of Heckscher and Ohlin by Samuelson over the years that it is now referred to as the Heckscher–Ohlin–Samuelson model.

Going forward, on issues of tariffs and trade policy Bhagwati is of the view that there are two commonly held assumptions in the tariff theory; either tariffs become a part of direct government expenditure or they are given as a subsidy to consumers who treat it as earned income. The result depends upon whether government consumption is in harmony with private consumption. If not, the implication of government consumption will differ from that of private consumption. As Bhagwati puts it in his 'The Pure Theory of International Trade', 'Subject to these ... specifications, the H.O.S model can be readily employed to work out a large number of formulae concerning the impact of tariff change on domestic and international terms of trade (and hence also on the absolute and relative shares in national income of each of the two classes of factors).'

Bhagwati then systematically takes us through his sections on technological change, changes in international demand, shifts in trade policy, discriminatory tariff changes, theorems in dynamics, and change in trade policy until he comes to a section on central limitations: intermediates and capital goods.

On the latter he laments 'the negligible dent made so far by intermediate and capital goods in the theoretical models employed by analysts of international trade'. 'More important,' he says, 'is the fact that a vast range of interesting problems, applicable to economics using intermediate and (produced) capital goods, cannot get within the range of analysis until the theorists get away from the traditional picture of primary factors and integrated processes of production (with the inevitable concomitant feature of trade in consumer goods).'

'What exactly does this mean?' a student asks.

It means that there are only primary factors like labour, raw materials, capital goods, and consumer goods in trade, and no intermediates.

Bhagwati then looks beyond 'the traditional multiplier analysis in Trade Theory which postulates the impact of exports and/or autonomous investment on the balance of payments and the levels of domestic output and employments'. However, there is another side to this in the event of excess capacity, when a country has to spend scarce foreign exchange to import raw materials. An extra unit of foreign exchange in such a case will add value in excess of the amount spent on intermediates, especially if the output of one industry becomes the input of another and so on. The sum of all the outputs will then give us a multiplier measure of the impact of an incremental amount of import on the total increase in output. In short, the role of imported intermediates or capital goods in breaking bottlenecks in domestic capacity utilization, especially in countries that are short of foreign exchange, is vital to an understanding of trade in the real world.

Thereafter, Bhagwati ranks various trade policies in terms of gains and losses to the trading countries. Of these, we shall mention only one—ranking of policies by the Samuelson criterion. This ranking looks at the proposition that *free trade is superior to any trade policy* from the standpoint of international advantage. It follows then that maximizing national advantage is a second-best option. As special cases of the above stated proposition, it also follows that *free trade is superior to no trade, free trade is superior to expanded trade, and free trade is superior to restricted trade.*

Finally, a number of sections are devoted to the welfare implications of different tariff and subsidy policies, and ranked based on different criteria.

In conclusion, Bhagwati believes that there is a growing trend towards the empirical verification of trade theories as well as an acceptance of the crucial role of intermediates and capital goods. Likewise, trade theories are increasingly concerned with the welfare implications of different policies and their measurement, especially in the context of planned economies. In short, trade theory is work-in-progress.

So far we have briefly examined some foundational aspects of trade theory and acknowledged Bhagwati's scholarship. We shall now discuss his ideas on tariff evasion and his signal contribution of what is known as 'immiserizing growth'.

Much of Bhagwati's work in the 1970s deals with what he calls 'directly unproductive, profit-seeking activities' or DUP. This is about *the theoretical analysis of tariff evasion*, which was pioneered by Bhagwati and B. Hansen in their paper titled 'A Theoretical Analysis of Smuggling' that was published in 1973. Numerous articles were written thereafter, including 'The General Equilibrium Theory of Effective Protection and Resource Allocation' authored by Bhagwati and T.N. Srinivasan, which appeared in *The Journal of International Economics* in 1973. There were other works as well, including the seminal work on *premium seeking* by Ann Krueger published in 1974 under the title 'The Political Economy of the Rent-Seeking Society'. From then on, there is much published on *tariff seeking* or lobbying for protectionist tariffs.

This whole area is grouped by Bhagwati under DUP activities. Examples are tariff evasion, premium seeking, and lobbying which 'are all privately profitable activities', yet their impact on direct output is zero. For instance, the difference between legal tariff-bearing imports and the illegal evasion of tariffs yields a monetary income, as does the premium on the sale of an import licence. The theoretical analysis of such DUP activities and their impact on welfare, both positive and negative, are the subject of Bhagwati's article titled 'Directly Unproductive, Profit-seeking (DUP) Activities' published in 1982.

Up went a hand. 'But isn't this common in India?'

It is quite common in India, as it is in other countries. Hence the importance of a rigorous theoretical analysis like the one presented by Bhagwati. We, however, shall not go into this further as it falls well beyond our scope. The students, however, would not allow me to drop it.

'There must be examples from the Indian experience?'

There were indeed many Indian examples, especially from the 1980s. There was one famous case where an ambitious industrialist was able to influence the government to drop the tariff on the import of machinery for the manufacture of polyester filament yarn to zero for one week. During this window, he imported enough equipment along with 'spares' not only to meet his licensed capacity but much more. The import duty was restored to its original level at the end of the week. The enormity of the profit can well be imagined. The output of the nylon yarn, which was in short supply in the country, shot up, thus laying the foundation for the largest

private sector company in India. The Hindi movie *Guru* depicts
this episode with greater colour.

The question raised by Bhagwati, however, remains. Is this a case of DUP activities that 'represent ways of making profit (i.e. income) by undertaking activities which are directly unproductive; that is, they yield pecuniary returns but do not produce goods or services'? Clearly though, after building productive capacity by beating the system through bribery or other means, our entrepreneur produced goods and services.

Bhagwati's answer would probably be that faulty policies or tariffs often lead to flawed market interventions and *directly unproductive* rent-seeking behaviour, which stems from a suboptimal form of economic organization.

To Bhagwati the touchstone of efficiently functioning markets would be a world free of tariffs. So has the behaviour of our entrepreneur led to greater welfare? The hint of an answer can be seen in the following quote. If 'there is an initially distorting tariff [the import duty on polyster yarn making machinery in our example was enormous] ... such tariff evasion may be welfare improving [even allowing for the fact that the illegality carries an extra, negative dimension]'. Bhagwati further classifies DUP activities into a number of categories and discusses their different welfare implications. The interested reader may refer to Bhagwati's article.

Moving on, it is widely held that Bhagwati is responsible for the current notion of 'immiserizing growth'. Bhagwati is known to have proposed the concept in his paper titled 'Immiserizing Growth: A Geometrical Note' published in 1958. 'Immiserizing growth' is defined as a situation where increased economic activity leads to a fall in the standard of living, especially where the use of resources like labour, land, and capital have an opportunity cost. The benchmark for judging such a situation would be a departure from perfectly functioning markets in a world free of tariffs. Such a departure would lead to rent-seeking behaviour.

'But how do you judge the example cited earlier?'

I would say that it was a case of 'immiserizing growth' in Bhagwati's terms. A high tariff on the import of machinery reduced to enable a particular entrepreneur to bring in tariff-free equipment and then raising it to bar competitors from doing the same clearly led to a monopoly situation. It was a suboptimal situation in the sense that the output of filament nylon yarn could have been much larger and delivered at competitive prices if competition had been encouraged. Immiserizing growth, however, can also take place in a closed economy, for example, where the ratio of labour to land is so adverse that agricultural output could actually be larger with less labour and some machinery—clearly a throwback to the Ricardian model. In India, this took the shape of smaller and smaller landholdings with the growth of landowning families. This caused output to drop well below its potential, until the onset of the green revolution of the 1960s. Further, with growing employment opportunities in the industry and service sectors, there has been a move towards contract farming by combining landholdings and the use of better seeds, fertilizers, and tractors, which has led to an improvement in agricultural output.

Other examples of immiserizing growth given by Bhagwati in his *In Defense of Globalization* (2004) talk of India's reliance on heavy industry in relation to light industry in the years after Independence. The former was capital-intensive while the latter was labour-intensive. The former also had to rely on massive import-substitution, which meant a huge outflow of foreign exchange in a situation where India's exports comprised largely of primary goods like jute, and cotton and textiles, the terms of trade for which were often adverse. This led to a regime of exchange controls and, in consequence, to a wide gap between the controlled price and open market price of foreign exchange. Light industry lagged behind and its products were hardly export-worthy. With a wide gap between imports and exports, India faced a major debt crisis by 1991.

In comparison, the East Asian Miracle economies mentioned earlier followed an export-led high-growth path from the 1960s onwards. This was based on a judicious mix of exports and import substitution, as discussed in an earlier chapter. What followed were high growth, high employment, and growing per capita income in an environment of reasonable macroeconomic stability. India's record until the 1990s was dismal: poor growth, low per capita incomes, much disguised unemployment, and a macroeconomic crisis in 1991. Further, autarkic policies on import substitution led to a high-cost economy and choked off export opportunities. It was a clear case of immiserizing growth.

In his fascinating book *India in Transition* (1993), Bhagwati gives a blow-by-blow account of why India stagnated through the 1950s to the early 1990s. Thereafter, with a major dose of reforms, inspired in no small measure by the collapse of the Soviet Union and its own economic compulsions, India was put on a high-growth path under Prime Minister Narasimha Rao with Dr Manmohan Singh as the finance minister.

'What were these reforms about?' a student asks.

We must remember that India was burdened with the 'licence permit raj'. This meant internal controls on capacity expansion or product diversification for both new and old projects. These were removed in one go in 1991, except on eighteen industries linked to city planning and pollution management. Barriers to entry on 'large' or 'dominant' firms under the Monopolies and Restrictive Trade Practices (MRTP) Act, 1969, were replaced by regulatory agencies like in the West to ensure free competition.

In another bold measure after the devaluation of the Indian rupee in July 1991, the finance minister declared the rupee 'partially convertible' in March 1992. Why 'partial'? You may wonder. This was because despite full convertibility on 'current account', there were different exchange rates for exporters and importers—really a measure to restrict the import of consumer goods. Furthermore, 40 per cent of the exchange earnings were used for essential imports like oil and fertilizers. Therefore, despite trade liberalization, there were three exchange rates in prevalence: one for exports and two for imports. In any event, it was a sea change from the earlier regime.

Alongside these changes, a new investor-friendly policy was announced in November 1991. This encouraged multinationals that could now invest up to 51 per cent in 'high-priority' industries and repatriate profits. With gradual relaxation, this saw a plethora of new projects in the 'white' goods and automobile sectors. In short, foreign direct investment flowed much more freely into India.

There was good news on the public sector front as well, which had so far been mostly regarded as a drain on the exchequer. Its domain was narrowed to eight from the earlier eighteen, namely to atomic energy, defence equipment, coal, petroleum, railways, and certain areas of mining. Many areas like aircraft manufacture, airlines, shipbuilding, and electric power were off the list. The next two decades saw a rapid rise in India's growth rates, which touched 8.7 per cent in 2009–10. What happened thereafter is a sad story of staggered reforms.

How do we sum up Bhagwati's contribution as an economist? I recognize that this is an impossible task. Yet, in brief, let us say that he has been a crusader for globalization, the theoretical justification for which is echoed in his earlier writings, particularly in his article 'The Pure Theory of International Trade'. Thereafter, his *In Defense of Globalization* sets out his arguments in a highly readable manner, peppered with his characteristic humour. In his later writings such as *Termites in the Trading System* (2008), Bhagwati has been highly critical of preferential trade agreements, which, he argues strongly, cut into the benefits of multilateral trade. In addition, though not blindly against protective tariffs, Bhagwati cautions that these should be time-bound measures.

It is no surprise that Bhagwati has been much sought after in the deliberations of GATT and WTO.[1]

[1] The General Agreement on Tariffs and Trade (GATT) came into existence in 1948. There was an overhang from the 1930s of protectionist measures, which were not addressed by the Bretton Woods institutions, namely the World Bank and the IMF. GATT lasted for forty-seven years and though its basic text remained the same, there were additions during the period such as 'plurilateral' voluntary memberships and agreements to reduce tariffs through a series of 'trade rounds'. The Uruguay Round of trade negotiations under GATT led to the establishment of the World Trade Organization (WTO), whose guiding principle is the foundation of a multilateral trading system. Although negotiated and signed by governments, its goal is to help producers of goods and services, exporters, and importers to conduct their business, while allowing governments to meet social and environmental objectives.

Conscience of the Economics Profession

Every child in the process of growing up has some indelible memories that shape the course of his or her life. Amartya Sen is someone who converted that burden into a gift for the poor and deprived of the world.[1]

Born in an old part of Dhaka in 1933, Sen began his education at an English missionary school at the age of three. Soon thereafter, his father Ashutosh, who taught chemistry at Dhaka University, had him sent to Santiniketan, also known as Visva-Bharati University, where young Amartya's maternal grandfather Kshitimohan taught Sanskrit. Sen's father sent him to Santiniketan as he sensed that Dhaka was a likely target of Japanese bombers during the war years. For Sen, the closeness to his grandfather turned out to be a blessing. Santiniketan was the abode of the great poet Rabindranath Tagore. Here, Sen was able to sit under the eucalyptus trees with his grandfather and listen to him speaking about the connection between

---

[1] Nasar's *Grand Pursuit* includes a brilliant chapter on Sen.

Sanskrit and Greek. Surely, Kshitimohan was convinced that his
grandson would carry forward the family's academic tradition.

Sen witnessed his first trauma in 1943 during the great Bengal
famine. The famine was believed to be the result of the indiffer-
ence of the British rulers to the plight of the poor rather than a
general crop failure. There was plenty of food stored by middle-
men in the name of helping the war effort while starving villagers
and fishermen streamed through Calcutta (now Kolkata) and the
neighbouring Santiniketan. Sen saw this misery first-hand at the
age of ten. He handed out packets of rice as allowed by his grandfather. Some years later, at college Sen was to reflect that only the
very poor and those of the lower castes suffered. An estimated three
million people died during the Bengal famine. Soon to follow
were the atrocities of Hindus on Muslims and vice versa at the
cusp of Independence and the Partition. Sen was on holiday at
their family home in Dhaka when he witnessed a gruesome scene.
A man who had been stabbed in the back by Hindu rioters and
was covered in blood lurched screaming towards their house. His
name was Kader Mia and before dying in hospital that day he
told Sen's father that he had come to the Hindu part of the town
looking for work since his family had no food. The connection
between extreme poverty and lack of choice was to inspire Sen's
philosophical exploration into the conflict between necessity
and freedom.

In 1951, Sen joined Presidency College in Calcutta, one of the
most prestigious in the country. There he was to read the works
of great economists like Marshall, John Hicks, and Samuelson,
but, most importantly, he read voraciously on other subjects and
participated in passionate debates with his Marxist and Stalinist
friends.

At the age of nineteen, Sen discovered a tiny growth in the pal-
ate of his mouth. It turned out to be cancerous. What followed
was a traumatic experience for him and his family, especially since
there were hardly any cancer hospitals in Calcutta. Sen read up

medical journals and found that at that time radiation was the standard treatment in Europe and America. Facing the possibility of death, he took matters in his own hands and located a radiologist who was willing to treat him. Over the span of a week, he received almost five times the recommended dosage. The cancer cells were defeated, but Sen had to undergo reconstructive surgery of the mouth some years later in England.

Back at Presidency College after his radiation treatment, Sen felt a certain elation having taken command of his own life in the face of overwhelming odds—this despite the horrific condition of his mouth and face post-radiation. According to Nasar's *Grand Pursuit*, Sen's personal suffering created in him a lasting empathy for those 'who were also hurting, voiceless and deprived'. He cleared his exams with a first division and won numerous prizes. Thereafter, he enrolled at Trinity College in Cambridge where he had the occasion to interact with scholars of a wide range of persuasions. Among them was the rather formidable Joan Robinson. She was his thesis supervisor, and Sen found her in frequent disagreement with his own views. Robinson would be much more in tune with the Soviet style of central planning with a focus on heavy industry, a model adopted by Nehru for India in the 1950s. Sen's thesis *The Choice of Techniques* (1960) was critical of his approach because technology was capable of being adapted to the size of the labour pool available and therefore a blind belief in the efficacy of heavy industry was against the basic principles of economics. This he shows through a formal analysis and numerous examples in his thesis.

It is ironic that while Robinson praised China's 'Great Leap Forward', Sen—as cited in Nasar's book—was to point out later that, sadly, between 15 million to 30 million Chinese had 'perished in the aftermath of forced collectivization'. That such a tragedy had not occurred in India after the Bengal famine, he attributed to India's democracy where information could travel freely from one corner of the country to another. On the subject of malnutrition and the lack of entitlements, however, Sen had much to say with reference to South Asia and sub-Saharan Africa.

It was in 1970 that Sen broke out of the Nehruvian mould of development economics, leaving behind a number of his colleagues including his brilliant classmate Sukhamoy Chakraborty to carry forward the Nehruvian flag. This remarkable phase in his career saw a shift towards welfare economics, which was marked by a number of path-breaking philosophical papers. At the same time, on the personal front Sen had to face some traumatic events—his father's death, the reconstructive surgery of his mouth, and a divorce from his wife from whom he had two young daughters. He had fallen madly in love with an Italian economist Era Colorni, with whom he would go on to spend the next thirteen years until her death in 1985.

Up went a hand and was followed by a question: 'Was Sen just a soft-hearted thinker or did he involve himself with hard economics?'

If by 'hard economics' you mean, for example, different approaches to equilibrium analysis and the use of mathematics, I must say that Sen was a master logician and logic goes deep to the root of mathematics. The difference was that instead of applying himself to the familiar areas of money, growth, and trade, Sen asked more fundamental questions: was the maximization of GDP by itself a sufficient condition for maximizing human welfare? Sen, in fact, argued that material prosperity alone in the shape of per capita income was not a complete measure of social well-being. Indeed his position stands contrary to a long tradition of utilitarian thinkers like Jeremy Bentham, John Rawls, and Hayek. Where his views would perhaps come close to Hayek's are on the question of the state's encroachment on the rights of individuals.

If you go back to the section on Hayek's battle with Keynes, you will find that the former doggedly protested against the centralization of power with the state to borrow and spend, even if it was for a temporary period till a recession—in this case, the

Great Depression—lifted. After the war, Hayek's philosophy was reflected in the Mont Pèlerin debates. At the core of these debates was whether government planning should override the plans of individuals, even though individual choice on whether to spend or save, according to Keynes, would not in a deep recession help to lift unemployment and the GDP. Whether Sen would go so far as to refute Keynes's solution given a deep crisis is doubtful, but there is no question that in principle he would support Hayek on the broader issue of the state interfering with the individual's freedom of choice.

The 1950s brought with them a different challenge: could any system of voting lead to results that reflected the preferences of individual citizens? No, said Kenneth Arrow, the American economist who proved beyond doubt that this was impossible. Hence came into being what was called the Arrow impossibility theorem. Sen was worried whether this theorem could be interpreted to support authoritarianism.

There were, of course, other theories where Utilitarians like Bentham spoke about welfare in terms of 'the greatest good for the greatest number'. Rawls who was mainly concerned with rights and believed that rights should take precedence over welfare was largely ignored by other economists. Then there was Vilfredo Pareto who argued that the optimum position for a society was where you could not make anyone better-off without making someone else worse-off. To this Sen responded with his article 'The Impossibility of the Paretian Liberal' published in 1970, where he showed that rights and welfare were both important but that there was a distinct possibility of a conflict between the two. Take the case of a father who defines his own welfare as extending to preventing his daughter from marrying a man of her choice—or, as has happened often in India, some group takes objection on the grounds of hurt feelings to the publication and sale of, say, Wendy Doniger's book on Hinduism. Likewise, miscreants destroyed M.F. Husain's paintings, claiming that the paintings had hurt religious sentiments. These were clearly examples of rights versus welfare. Pareto optimality here came into conflict with free choice as a right.

'But this is a very important point made by Sen. We confront this problem every day,' observes a student.

Sen had indeed made an important point. Where do we draw the line between individual rights and social welfare?

Sen's preoccupation thus extended to tackling Arrow's impossibility theorem. In his path-breaking work entitled *Collective Choice and Social Welfare* (1970), Sen looked critically at Arrow's axioms and found that one of them rather arbitrarily ruled out comparisons of well-being between different individuals. In other words, while Arrow's theorem allowed for the ordering of individual preferences, there was no measure of their intensity or interpersonal comparison of utility. Sen found that if such comparisons were permitted, then the impossibility condition would no longer hold. This finding spawned a considerable amount of research on the subject.[2]

By the 1980s, Sen returned to his earlier concerns about poverty, hunger, and starvation. The result was his 1981 study for the International Labour Organization entitled *Poverty and Famines: An Essay on Entitlement and Deprivation.*

To begin with, Sen takes us through the different concepts of poverty. B. Rowntree defines the biological approach to 'primary poverty' of families in his *Poverty: A Study in Town Life* (1901) as 'that state where their total earnings are insufficient to obtain the minimum necessities for the maintenance of merely physical efficiency'. The focus here is on survival for work efficiency.

The problem with this definition is that climatic conditions, work habits, and physical characteristics of the population of different regions determine the nutritional requirements, which

[2] See also Anand's entry on Sen in *The New Palgrave Dictionary of Economics* (2008).

makes it difficult to define them precisely. Yet there is no denying that the physical stature of the people in the US, Europe, and Japan has grown significantly over time with better nutrition.

However, when it comes to different 'groups and regions', there is a certain arbitrariness involved in defining a minimal nutritional standard. There have, of course, been attempts to reconcile *nutritional* requirements with *food* requirements by using the programming approach to minimize the cost of a specified nutritional requirement. This does not work in practice because, for instance, nothing in most parts of India will be acceptable as a substitute for onions even if it has greater nutritional value. The same applies to soya bean as a substitute for meat. Does this mean that the biological approach has no value? Certainly not. As Sen points out in his *Poverty and Famines* that 'while the concept of nutritional requirements is a rather loose one, there is no particular reason to suppose that the concept of poverty must itself be clear-cut and sharp'. Then again, to determine whether a person is getting adequate nutrition, one need not go through the route of examining his income level. One can just as well determine this through sample surveys of the 196 consumption bundles of different segments of the population. While malnutrition relates to only one aspect of poverty, there is no denying that it occupies a central place, especially for developing countries.

This brings us to the idea that poverty has also to do with income inequality and that the transfer of wealth from the rich to the poor can have an impact on it. While Sen concedes that there is merit in, say, looking at the bottom 10 per cent in relation to the rest of society, neither poverty nor inequality can really be included in the empire of the other. While poverty and inequality may be associated with each other, they are not conceptually equivalent.

Sen then goes on to talk about *relative deprivation* where he juxtaposes *feelings* of deprivation with *conditions* of deprivation. Shekhar

Gupta described this well for a changing India in his article titled 'National Interest' (2014):

The real story of socio-economic change in India is hidden in the data on evolving food habits. The NSSO (National Sample Survey Organisation) also tells you our per capita grain consumption has been declining (net of rural and urban). It fell 1.3 per cent CAGR (compound annual growth rate) between 2005 and 2010 and is declining further. But watch what is increasing: milk and milk products (1.5), mutton (2.4), fish (5.0), edible oil (5.3), eggs (10.6) and chicken (hold your breath, at 18.4). Don't blame just Punjabis, all of India is becoming a *kukkad* nation now. But more seriously, we Indians, fed up of mere grain, now want better quality foods: fruits, vegetables and, most importantly, oil and proteins. Indians, across social classes, are now eating on the basis of their preferences and junking the old notion of more [of the same].

On the issue of feelings, Sen quotes from Smith's *The Theory of Moral Sentiments*: 'A linen shirt, for example, is, strictly speaking, not a necessity of life. The Greeks and Romans lived, I suppose, very comfortably though they had no linen. But in the present times, through the greater part of Europe, a creditable day-labourer would be ashamed to appear in public without a linen shirt.'

Sen then rounds off this part of the argument by saying:

It is certainly true that with economic development there are changes in the notion of what counts as deprivation and poverty, and there are changes also in the ideas as to what should be done. But while these two types of changes are interdependent and also intertemporally correlated with each other, neither can be *defined* entirely in terms of the other.

Thereafter, Sen raises two questions. First, how to find a common standard of necessities since they would vary from society to society. As this leads to the calories versus commodity debate, in most cases it is possible to work with a hybrid approach. For example, 'amounts of calories, proteins, housing, schools, hospital beds—some of the components being pure characteristics, while others are unabashed commodities'.

Second, how to aggregate the deprivations of different individuals into an overall index? This would require some scaling of deprivations and would not be without a measure of arbitrariness. That, however, should not detract from the importance of the exercise.

Sen accordingly gives us two axioms H and I, from which he derives 'a quite general format of the poverty measure'. H is the percentage of people below some agreed poverty line, and I is 'the proportionate amount of absolute income deprivation', that is, how much on the average below the poverty line. By imposing those two axioms on the weighted sum of the income gaps, Sen derives a precise measure of poverty. This is shown below:

$$P = H \{I + (1 - I) G\}$$

where P is the measure of poverty and G is the Gini coefficient. *'What is the Gini coefficient?' a student asks.*

The Gini coefficient is a commonly used measure of the inequality of income distribution. Its formula is as follows:

$$G = 1 + \frac{1}{n} - \frac{2}{n^2 \bar{y}}[y_1 + 2y_2 + 3y_3 + \cdots + ny_n]$$

where $y_1, ..., y_n$ are individual incomes in decreasing order of size,
    $\bar{y}$ is the mean income, and
    n is the number of individuals.

In Sen's words, 'Thus, the measure P is a function of H (reflecting the number of poor), I (reflecting the poverty gap), and G (reflecting the inequality of income distribution below the poverty line). The last captures the aspect of "relative deprivation".'

It also shows that 'the question of distribution remains relevant even when incomes *below* the poverty line are considered'. This is especially relevant to the subject of starvation and famines.

'Famines,' as Sen points out, 'imply starvation, but not vice versa.' Most importantly, 'starvation implies poverty, but not vice versa'. In other words, no matter what the relative deprivation, starvation is characterized by *absolute dispossession*.

Sen then takes us through a brief history of famines from ancient times, through medieval times, to modern times in different parts of the world. One of the important conclusions is that despite adequate food being available in a country and the world, there can exist pockets of acute starvation. This leads to Sen's entitlement approach wherein if a person or a community does not have the 'ability to command enough food', it can suffer starvation. The entitlement approach is applied to five case studies: the great Bengal famine; the Ethiopian famine; the drought and famine in Sahel, which lies between the Sahara Desert and the African tropical rainforests; and the famine in Bangladesh, which resulted from the floods of 1974. In conclusion, Sen discusses some general issues of deprivation in the context of entitlement systems.

In a later work titled *Development as Freedom* (1999), which is considered a classic, Sen pulls together a number of his concepts developed earlier and goes on to explore the many ways in which freedom is linked to economic development. So let us discuss some key instrumental freedoms that extend 'the overall freedom people have to live the way they would like to live'. These, according to Sen, are: (a) political freedoms, (b) economic facilities, (c) social opportunities, (d) transparency guaranties, and (e) protective security.

The first refers to the liberties and rights associated with well-functioning democracies. They include the opportunity to vote in legislators and to debate, dissent, and criticize those in authority. Furthermore, it presumes that the existence of the press and media is free from controls.

The second relates to the economic opportunities available to individuals in a well-functioning market where there is freedom to use national resources for production, consumption, and exchange. Here while the aggregate growth rate of an economy is important, it is equally important to ensure that each individual gets a fair share of his entitlement. In other words, the way additional aggregate income is distributed is of great significance. Sen also points towards the access to finance, which small firms are often denied during a credit crunch.

'But how can you divert funds from a firm's earning in a market economy?'

When firms make profits, the government is entitled to tax them within certain norms. In fact, when firms do better, tax revenues go up and vice versa during a slump. In either event, governments are supposed to spend on what Sen calls entitlements in the form of healthcare, education, nutrition, indeed the whole social sector. For Sen, these entitlements are as important as keeping the growth rate up. As we have discussed earlier, during a slowdown in the economy, deficit-financing is usually undertaken so that the social sector does not suffer.

The third is *social opportunities*, which refer to the different ways in which education and healthcare affect private lives in terms of the absence of morbidity and a longer lifespan. All these freedoms reinforce each other. Sen gives the example of how literacy improves participation in economic activity. Let me share my own experience at DCM Limited. We had a joint venture with Toyota Motors of Japan for the manufacture of light commercial vehicles. The production commenced in 1985. All the workers on the assembly line were from the neighbouring villages and the managers were company-trained engineers from DCM Limited. There were, of course, a few personnel from Japan in the initial period.

When assembly was about to begin, the Japanese asked us for the instruction sheet. We showed them the production manual neatly typed out in English. They asked us if our workers could read English. We were baffled. It turned out that they wanted one page, neatly printed with not more than three instructions in Hindi stuck on each machine. About half the workers could read Hindi; the others were given special classes. This was our first lesson in how to raise the productivity on the shop floor. India, of course, has come some way since then.

Sen further talks about the impact of literacy on quality control, which is extremely important for exports, and the ability to participate meaningfully in the political process through reading newspapers and written communication.

The fourth freedom is what Sen calls *transparency guarantees*. It is about mutual trust in daily transactions. For instance, legal contracts cannot be drawn up each time a person wishes to buy, say, a medicine or a bag of flour. There should be enough openness and trust among people to ensure that a customer is not short-changed. This is a very real problem in India, where food articles are often adulterated. All articles on sale should clearly state the contents on the package. Transparency guarantees thus have a direct link with the ability to read, the prevention of corruption, as well as to general health.

Finally, *protective security* is important because however well a society does, there will always be people on the margins of subsistence. There would thus have to be institutional arrangements such as unemployment benefits and ad hoc relief during famines or floods. One could extend the idea to cover the protection of minorities from the high-handedness of the majority as well as women against atrocities by men.

Throughout the discussion Sen emphasizes the importance of the interconnections of the different freedoms. Education, for example, should bring about a cultural change such that cheating is looked down upon and transparency guarantees reinforced. Likewise, if economic facilities lead to improving the growth rate and the material prosperity of the population, they will reinforce the need for better education and healthcare.

'*How would Sen explain the fact that many educated people do not get jobs?*'

Sen is all for higher growth and globalization. And high growth is directly connected to greater employment. However, the employability of people is equally connected to education, as Sen argues. The question of educated people not getting jobs, though linked to slow growth, is also dependent on the right kind of skill development as well as the quality of education.

On the macro plane, Sen gives the example of Japan during the Meiji era which lasted from 1868 to 1911. During this period, Japan's literacy rate was higher than that of Europe. This was so even though industrialization had not yet taken root in Japan unlike in Europe. Yet by the time of the Great War of 1914, Japan had become an industrial and military power to reckon with. Much credit for this goes to the focus on literacy and human development, which preceded industrialization. The other Asian Miracle nations followed Japan's example especially in regard to human development.

On India and China, Sen held the view that while China's reforms towards a market-oriented economy began in 1979 and India's in 1991, China has outpaced India in industrial production by a huge margin. Much credit for this goes to China's commitment to healthcare and education during the pre-reform period. On India, Sen says:

[I]n contrast, India had a half-illiterate adult population when it turned to marketization in 1991, and the situation is not much improved today.

... The social backwardness of India, with its elitist concentration on higher education and massive negligence of school education, and its substantial neglect of basic health care, left that country poorly prepared for a widely shared economic expansion.

... [T]he relevance of the radically different levels of social preparedness in China and India for widespread market-oriented development is worth noting.

This brings us to the often-heard argument that democracy is a luxury for countries at an early stage of development and that there is a trade-off between rapid development and the messiness of democratic freedoms. The examples often cited are of

Singapore and China. Singapore certainly developed fast under the benevolent dictatorship of Lee Kuan Yew, but a generation later it is still not a free society. China has certainly grown rapidly but the question of whether it will move towards democratic freedoms is open to doubt. Japan and South Korea are counterexamples, which along with the other East Asian Miracle economies have progressed materially in large measure because of democratic freedoms.

Sen then raises a rather fundamental question in his *Development as Freedom* (1999): whether there is really any substantial difference between development analysis that focuses (as Lewis and many others choose to do) on 'the growth of output per head' (such as GNP per capita), and a more fundamental concentration on expanding human freedom.

Lewis (whom we have talked about earlier) points out that the two approaches are closely linked. Sen asks why then do we need a 'focal concentration' on freedom.

Sen argues that there are two aspects to freedom. One relates to the *processes of decision-making* and the other to the *opportunities to achieve valued outcomes*. Outcomes are best understood as maximizing consumption or per capita income, normally a function of economic growth. The processes of decision-making, on the other hand, involve social choice such as participation in political discussion and voting. Importantly, while the latter may contribute indirectly to economic development, it has to be seen primarily as an *end* in itself.

For greater clarity, let us take an example. How many of you have heard of Chetan Bhagat? Nearly all the hands went up. You may know that he graduated from an IIT and then studied at IIM Ahmedabad. You may also know that after working in a bank for some time, he became a fulltime author. By opting out of a bank job, which clearly gave him a decent and secure income, he made the rather risky choice of becoming a writer. The former would have contributed to his physical comfort as well as to the economy.

The latter may also have contributed to the economy, but most importantly, it contributed to his sense of well-being and personal fulfilment. Note that his education greatly widened his freedom of choice. Expanding human freedoms thus becomes an end, going well beyond economic prosperity.

There are other examples of highly qualified individuals returning from abroad and starting their own non-government organizations in order to contribute their skills and experience to philanthropic work. Their efforts may not add to GDP directly, but could make a difference to the social welfare. The key point is that for such people their education gave them the freedom of choice. Their success could mark a turning point in not just the economy but also the welfare of society.

Let us take a look now at the other side of the social spectrum. Choices are restricted for those who lack an education and have to live on the margins of subsistence. Their existence remains 'brutish' until the state can provide assistance in the form of healthcare, schooling, and nourishment. Children here are the greatest sufferers, especially girls who are at the receiving end of not just economic deprivation but also social prejudice. They are denied a fair share of food entitlement in comparison to the male child. Their very existence is often considered a burden by their families, which may even result in cases of female infanticide. Equally shocking, families resort to female foeticide in collusion with their doctor. In most cases the mother has no choice. Such a practice is especially prevalent among the newly prosperous classes in the towns and in the farming communities of Haryana and Punjab. In consequence, the male-to-female ratio remains skewed against females. According to Sen, many such social ills cannot be tackled by a rise in per capita income alone. They require a cultural change related to broad-based education.

Sen goes on to point out the difference between 'human capital and human capability'. As we noted earlier, Japan and later the East Asian Miracle economies placed great emphasis on the development of human capital. What this meant was not just good schooling but also skill development, including the ability to absorb the basic elements of technology. This led to the enhancement of productivity on different kinds of capital equipment. Hence the term 'human capital'. According to Sen, this narrower concept 'fits into the more inclusive perspective of human capability, which can cover both the direct and indirect consequences of human abilities'.

For a fuller appreciation of human capabilities, Sen points towards: (a) their direct relevance to the well-being and freedom of people, (b) their indirect role through influencing social change, and (c) their indirect role through influencing economic production.

In his various lectures in India, Sen often reminds us of the state of human development in Sri Lanka and Bangladesh, which with the exception of Kerala have outpaced the rest of India in terms of longevity, the condition of the girl child, schooling, and the avoidance of morbidity. Sen has written extensively on the human conditions in South Asia and sub-Saharan Africa with the result that international bodies have taken initiatives on various fronts.

Finally, we must make a mention of the great Pakistani economist Mahbub ul Haq, who was at one point Sen's colleague at Cambridge University. As adviser to the United Nations Development Programme, Haq initiated the Human Development Report as its project director and gathered together eminent economists including Sen and Meghnad Desai to prepare it. Thereafter, Haq's and Sen's names have been associated with what is known as the Human Development Index, which includes a number of parameters we have alluded to earlier. This index is published periodically and ranks the world's nations in descending order. India unfortunately ranks rather poorly.

❧

Sen won the Nobel Prize for welfare economics in 1998. It is no wonder that Solow, the American economist and an earlier recipient of the Nobel Prize, called Sen the 'conscience of our profession'.[3]

[3] Solow referred to Sen as the 'conscience of our profession' in 1994, after the latter was elected the president of the American Economic Association.

Reality versus Theory

One thing is true—economists can differ vehemently unlike, say, physicists. The same set of facts does not necessarily lead to the same conclusions in the field of economics. The earlier chapters have discussed many such instances. Yet economics is regarded as the 'emperor' of all social sciences. That is because despite accommodating differing social values and ideologies, it lends itself to rigorous mathematical analysis or the scientific method. Is this a fault? Let us see this in the context of the twenty-first century.

If we recall, the Keynesian halo was beginning to dim roughly thirty years after the death of Keynes. Until then most economies of the industrialized world were committed to the Keynesian prescription of using budget deficits to ensure full employment and they indeed prospered as never before. By and large, the growth rates were high and inflation as well as unemployment were kept under control.

Then with the oil shock in 1974 came the first wave of disillusionment when economies began to stagnate because of a massive oil price rise triggered by the organization of the petroleum-exporting countries. This led to stagnation accompanied by inflation, which according to Keynesian economics was impossible. Keynesians believed that there was always a trade-off between high inflation and low unemployment. Despite Samuelson's efforts to rescue Keynes by explaining this as a supply-side problem, the tide had begun to turn. By the time of the second oil shock in 1978, it had turned completely in favour of the monetarists. Milton Friedman and the Chicago School (the fresh water economists as opposed to the salt water ones on the East and West coasts) became the leading lights of government policy, notably in the era of Margaret Thatcher in Britain and Ronald Reagan in the US. Keynes had his thirty years after the War and Friedman and his followers had their thirty years until the Great Recession of 2008, albeit punctuated by periods of high unemployment.

There is a history to this, which Raghuram Rajan beautifully captures in his much lauded book *Fault Lines* (2010). In fact, Rajan was the first to predict the Great Recession.

You will recall from earlier chapters that the oil crisis of the 1970s had triggered an inflationary cycle, which despite some ups and downs lasted well into the early years of 2000s. The prices of houses, in consequence, registered a steady increase. According to Rajan, this affected the middle classes badly, notably the wage earners whose real wages had declined or remained constant. There were thus political compulsions during the Bill Clinton and George Bush administrations to make housing accessible to those earning low incomes. Rajan succinctly explains in *Fault Lines* why the rich became richer and the wage earners became poorer between 1975 and 2005. He attributes this to the inadequacy of high-school diplomas in dealing with the requirements of new technologies in higher-paying jobs and to the rising costs of college education. Since fixing the high costs of college education would be a long-drawn process, the politicians looked at short-term solutions by tampering with the financial system in order to make housing loans accessible to the poor.

To this end the government created two institutions: the Federal National Mortgage Association (FNMA or Fannie Mae) and the Federal Home Loan Mortgage Corporation (also known as Freddie Mac). These institutions were a hybrid of private and public enterprise and were exempt from paying 'state and local income taxes'. Furthermore, they had a direct line of credit from the US treasury at just above the treasury rate. Their mandate was to support housing finance and they did just this by buying mortgages from the banks and encouraged them to make more mortgage loans. Freddie Mac and Fanny Mae then bundled these loans into packages and issued mortgage-backed securities that were guaranteed against default. As Rajan says, 'They also started borrowing directly from the market and investing in mortgaged-backed securities underwritten by other banks.' This process spread rapidly through the banking system not only in the US but also in Europe and Britain. The going was great given the low cost of financing triggered by Freddie Mac and Fannie Mae, and this was to last as long as the housing prices kept rising. Once they began to decline, the situation turned grim.

According to Robert Skidelsky, the author of the incisive book on Keynes titled *Keynes: The Return of the Master* (2010), global bank debt came to be perched on a fragile base of assets in the form of house prices in America in 2007-8. This happened because banks in their quest for more business were making loans to sub-prime mortgage borrowers, that is, those who were unlikely to pay back. Consequently, when prices of houses began to fall, these loans began to show up as unsecured assets on the banks' balance sheets. What is incredible is that the loans covered more than the market value of the houses in the belief that housing prices would continue to rise as they had in the past. Since many banks were loaded with such securities and they could not determine how much their assets were worth, they stopped lending to each other. This led to a general credit crunch. As banks began to fail—some as large as Lehman Brothers—the stock markets followed suit and a worldwide slump followed by 2009.

'How could banks be so stupid?' a student asks with a look of surprise.

The banks clearly could not anticipate the consequences of their actions, as we shall see in a moment.

At the heart of the problem was 'securitization', which means putting together individual mortgages and cutting them into smaller pieces as required by investors. The originating bank then bundled them and sold them, and they travelled from one bank to another. Ostensibly, the risk of lending to sub-prime borrowers was spread between securities of differing riskiness. To top it, all credit-rating agencies like Moody's and Standard and Poor's rated most of them as AAA.

Let us take an example to understand this with greater clarity. There was this belief that all risks are measurable. For example, life insurance companies measure the risk of lending, on which their premiums are based rather accurately because they have reliable data on life expectancy. In a sense they can extrapolate from existing data which is 'a statistical reflection of the past'. Now imagine providing insurance on every kind of risk like credit risk, market risk, political risk, the risk of losing your reputation, or the risk of a major fire breaking out. Could these risks be calculated on actuarial principles? Obviously not.

Unfortunately, the chairpersons and boards of most banks did not understand the mathematics of risk management. Their whizz-kids put together models based on the familiar normal distribution or the Gaussian bell curve. They used this to establish a range of probabilities within which future events will occur. Most data points were clustered towards the middle.

Rare events or *Black Swans* that are found at the tail end of the curve tended to be ignored. Further, there was a belief that the risk attached to each asset was independent of the other. Consequently, the aggregate risk of holding many assets was lower because the risks unique to each asset would cancel each other out.

The models ignored the possibility that the risk of holding each asset could be correlated to the others, as happens in upswings and downswings. This is exactly what happened in the sense that a certain herd behaviour took over in the face of uncertainty. Furthermore, since these instruments travelled between continents in a globalized world, what started in the US spread to Britain and Europe.

If we were to go back to where it all began, prior to 1999 the US law forbade retail banks from undertaking investment activities like guaranteeing or selling securities. This condition was relaxed. The Clinton administration decided to deregulate credit default swaps and later the Securities and Exchange Commission permitted banks to raise their ratio of total liabilities to net worth from 10:1 to 30:1. Without going into a blow-by-blow account of what happened thereafter, suffice it to say that the Western banks were crippled by swallowing toxic securities. Banks in Asia, including India and Russia, were spared the trauma.

Where were the economists during this period? What did they have to say? The profession was divided between the Friedmanesque and the Keynesians who now called themselves the New Classical and the New Keynesian economists respectively. The leading light of the New Classical school was Robert Lucas, a former pupil of Friedman. Lucas gave rise to a new school of thought known as 'rational expectations', which he introduced in *Rational Expectations and Econometric Practice* (1981), the volume he co-edited with T.J. Sargent.

In brief, this was a take off from Friedman who believed that the future was 'probabilistic' rather than merely 'uncertain' as Keynes had proposed, and since economic agents learnt from past mistakes, they would not keep repeating them. Friedman believed that future risks were calculable and that government intervention could never improve upon the decisions of individual agents in free markets. Further, he changed the definition of full employment to mean not the absence of spare capacity but that rate of employment at which there would be no inflation. He called it the 'natural rate' of employment. Lucas took these concepts to their logical conclusion.

The New Keynesians, notably Joseph Stiglitz,[1] in the meantime proposed that information is never perfect but asymmetric. What this means is that buyers and sellers seldom have the same information to begin with, and therefore it takes time before markets can clear and stocks can come to their normal level. During this intervening period, governments have a role to play in restoring the economy to full employment.

Lucas would say based on the *rational expectations theory* that economic agents have perfect information and therefore prices and wages would adjust instantaneously, as would the prices of all goods and services. It follows that there would be no real difference between the long run and the short run because people have perfect information about the past and present and make efficient use of it to predict future events. As a result, they would always be at their preferred position. The need for government intervention would therefore be zero. Then how would one explain recurring business cycles? Lucas and his followers would say that periods of high growth and recessions are a *natural* response to events such as the oil shock or a cluster of new inventions, that is, changes in the rate of technological progress. Governments, therefore, should be kept out of the loop.

The 2008 crisis, as Skidelsky puts it, was 'a crisis of symmetric ignorance, not asymmetric information'. It showed both the New Classicals and the New Keynesians in a poor light. In earlier years, both Stiglitz and Lucas were recipients of the Nobel Prize.

---

[1] The works that are important to mention here are: 'Information and Competitive Price Systems' co-authored by Grossman and Stiglitz (1976), 'Equilibrium in Product Markets with Imperfect Information' by Stiglitz (1979); 'Financial Market Imperfections and Productivity Growth' co-authored by Greenwald, Kohn, and Stiglitz (1990); and 'Asymmetric Information in Credit Markets and Its Implications for Macro-economics' co-authored by Stiglitz and Weiss (1992).

When an amount of USD 600 billion was put into the economy during the Bush administration, Lucas (being a neoclassical economist) approved of it saying that a cash stimulus was just what was needed overlooking the New Classical position that market economies do not need to be stimulated. They are self-adjusting in the face of shocks. On the other hand, Paul Krugman, a Keynesian, argued in favour of a fiscal stimulus and government spending to lift the economy out of the recession. The debate continued.

'But what would Keynes have said?'

For one, Keynes would have rejected the idea that future risks are calculable. He would have said that uncertainty about the future cannot be reduced to a probability calculation as it has many more variables than a projection of past and present experiences. This was supported by his belief that human beings are not entirely rational as argued by the Chicago School (a neoclassical school of economic thought, the notable economists belonging to which are Gary Becker, Ronald Coase, Eugene Fama, Friedman, Lucas, and so on) but part rational and part emotional. In consequence, they are not immune from a certain herd behaviour.

Furthermore, Keynes would never have accepted that people possess the information required to equilibrate markets instantaneously—a belief held by the New Classicals. The New Keynesians would go along with the rational expectations hypothesis generally, but would allow for a short time lag before reaching equilibrium.

Next Keynes would argue that aggregate demand failure follows from uncertainty about the future emanating from collective psychological behaviour, which determines the propensity to consume, liquidity preference, and market sentiment. Macroeconomics thus cannot be built on a base of microeconomic optimization data as proposed by mainstream economists.

Finally, Keynes would reject Say's Law that supply creates its own demand as is widely believed by mainstream economists who argue that growth depends on technological progress and the breaking of supply bottlenecks. Growth, Keynes would hold, is driven by aggregate demand since technological progress stimulates demand and demand stimulates growth.

On the global front, it is worth noting that the Bretton Woods System of Keynes gave way in roughly 1980 to the Washington Consensus System. Tables 1 and 2 give a comparison of the two.

Table 1   Bretton Woods ('Golden Age') System

Objective	Instrument(s)	Responsible Authority
Full employment	Demand management (mainly fiscal)	National governments
Balance-of-payments adjustment	Pegged but adjustable exchange rates (capital controls)	IMF
Promotion of international trade	Tariff reductions, etc.	GATT
Economic development	Official assistance	The World Bank

Source: Skidelsky (2010: 116).

Table 2   Washington Consensus System

Objective	Instrument(s)	Responsible Authority
Price stability	Interest rate policy	National central bank, ECB for Eurozone
Balance-of-payments adjustment	Floating exchange rates	
Promotion of international trade	Tariff reductions, etc.	ITO, WTO (since 1995)
Economic development	Loans	Private lending, The World Bank

Source: Skidelsky (2010: 117).

It is clear that one reflected the belief that the global economy needed political and institutional support, while the other was based on the theory of self-regulating markets. Both systems fell short of expectations.

So where are we after seven years of the Great Recession of 2008-9? The US is showing green shoots of growth but has still not been able to restore its economy to the pre-recession level. Europe continues to be in a low growth cycle and the condition of Greece is dire. However, what defies conventional wisdom is that the inflation rate is falling in most countries. It is less than 1 per cent in the Euro zone and so is the average growth rate. It is a reverse problem now. Instead of stagflation, the bugbear of the 1970s, we now seem to be heading for stagnation with deflation.

In the third quarter of 2015, China went into a downward spiral: its stock markets crashed. The yuan depreciated against the USD, thus adding to the contagion effect on the rest of the world.

'So what is the state of economic theory?' asks a student.

Well, mainstream economists, whether fresh water or salt water, failed to anticipate the Great Recession and sadly offer no new tools to foresee the next major crisis, whenever it may occur. In fact, they appear to be groping for corrective solutions even in the aftermath of 2008.

Desai, however, provides an alternative approach in his very readable recent book *Hubris* (2015). The gist of Desai's argument is best offered in his own words:

The alternative explanation I have advanced in terms of a dynamic dis-equilibrium model of capitalism, using the ideas of Marx, Schumpeter, Wicksell and Hayek, has the merit of being able to weave together a global story with real and financial factors interplaying their roles against a background of political changes. Demographic factors also come into play differently in the first Keynesian boom of 1945–70 as compared to the later boom of 1992-2007. It would be a challenge to build a formal econometric model which can encompass these elements but it is not impossible. We have techniques of time series analysis which have rigorous ways of separating trends and cycles, and some which can pinpoint the frequency at which the maximum variability in the data is concentrated. Thus to spot a four- or ten-year cycle in the data or to locate whether a longer 40- or 50-year cycle can explain variability in the data is not beyond our statistical toolkit.

The thinkers Desai has alluded to have been discussed in earlier chapters. It is noteworthy that none of them celebrated the neoclassical style equilibrium where demand and supply meet or even sub-full employment equilibria proposed by Keynes. Likewise, they would have rejected the monetarist notion of equilibrium based on zero inflation, irrespective of its impact on employment on the assumption that the economy would be self-correcting.

They believed rather in long-term business cycles of the kind proposed by Nikolai Kondratieff—that they could last 40 to 50 years within which or outside of which there could be shorter-term cycles.

A rather plausible reason for such a phenomenon is put forward by Schumpeter who argues that major technological breakthroughs or innovations, the preserve of entrepreneurs as he calls them, do not happen in rhythmic cycles; that innovations lead to the creation of new markets and upswings in the economy. The steam engine leading to the discovery of the railways, for example, touched off a boom that lasted a good sixty years and within that was the parallel innovation of the steamship followed later by automobiles, aeroplanes, computers, and the software revolution. We see small innovations riding on the back of earlier ones in our daily lives, but large game changers do not have a predictable time frame—hence long-term cycles.

There is, however, a recent book by Piketty called *Capital in the Twenty-First Century* (2013) which is hard to ignore. It is voluminous in size, but I will try to present Piketty's central argument in brief. Its two nodal points are Capital (wealth) and Income, the behaviour of which he has studied empirically over two centuries for a number of countries. In the context of the US and Europe, the following two figures make an important statement.

The U-shaped graphs indicate that income inequality dropped significantly between 1945–50 and 1970–80 and then rose to the level of 1930 in the case of the US and above that level in Europe. While Piketty does not seem to mention it, these years of low

Figure 1 Income Inequality in the US, 1910–2010

Source: Piketty (2013).

Note: The top decile share in the US national income dropped from 45–50 per cent in the 1910s–1920s to less than 35 per cent in the 1950s (this is the fall documented by Kuznets); it then rose from less than 35 per cent in the 1970s to 45–50 per cent in the 2000s–2010s.

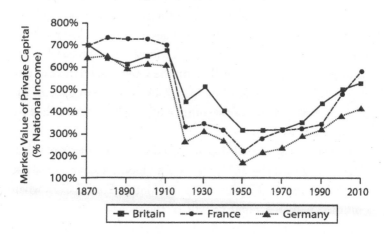

Figure 2 The Capital/Income Ratio in Europe, 1870–2010

Source: Piketty (2013).

Note: The aggregate private wealth was worth about six to seven years of the national income in Europe in 1910, between two and three years in 1950, and between four and six years in 2010.

income inequality and high growth coincide with the Keynesian decades. But more to the point what Piketty calls 'an absolutely crucial transformation is ... that the return of high capital/income ratios over the past few decades can be explained in large part by the return to a regime of relatively slow growth'. He believes that 'the risk of a divergence in the distribution of wealth is very high' when the rate of economic growth is low. This is because slow growth itself creates conditions in which 'inherited wealth grows faster than output and income'—a reason being that the return on higher saving from the income of the wealthy is greater than the growth rate of the economy.

He calls this 'the fundamental force of divergence' denoted by $r > g$ (where r stands for the annual average rate of return on capital, including profits, dividends, interest, rents, and other income from capital expressed as a percentage of its total value, while g stands for the rate of growth of the economy). This, Piketty believes, 'sums up the overall logic of my conclusions'.

What we have therefore is an exhaustive empirical study of the divergence of wealth and incomes of nations over a long time span well into the twenty-first century. The implications are multifold, perhaps throwing light on the recent experiences of tensions within nations spreading to regions in different parts of the globe. However, there are two other studies worth noting that are described below.

Going by conventional wisdom based on US estimates of world population growth by 2050, we have a gloomy scenario of a rise from 7.3 billion to 9.7 billion. As per Martin Ford (2015), when combined with the rapid growth of robots and artificial intelligence, this creates a scary picture of mass unemployment in the foreseeable future. However, in *The Rise and Fall of Nations* (2016), Ruchir Sharma presents a contrasting scenario where, he argues, with credible evidence that the growth of world population is slowing down with most emerging nations, including India and China, reaching close to replacement levels. Most industrial nations of the West as well as Japan and Russia have gone below replacement levels with the US on the borderline. The gives a skewed scenario of slowing population growth with a rising percentage of old people above the age of sixty-five and a declining working-age population between the ages of fifteen and sixty-four. This will inevitably slow down the growth rate of the GDP which results from enough working-age people, their education, and training. The responsibility on the state of looking after old people through welfare schemes will rise, thus placing a growing burden on the working-age population. In this background, 'the rise of robots' should be a support to the declining working-age population rather than a cause of unemployment. The future need not be so gloomy as foreseen by Malthus, especially with land now being able to support a declining population.

Speaking of the present state of economic theory, we have seen the tussle amongst mainstream economists as well as an off-stream invocation to the ideas of economists long past. Then there is Piketty's thesis of the divergence between the rate of the growth of wealth and that of national income 'as a fundamental force' along with Ford's and Sharma's differing visions of the future.

While the future is hard to predict with certainty, there is no doubt that it will be exciting with plenty of space for the evolution of new economic ideas.

Bibliography

Akamatsu, K. 1961. 'A Theory of Unbalanced Growth in the World Economy', *Weltwirtschaftliches Archiv*, 86(2): 196–207.

Anand, S. 2008. 'Sen, Amartya (Born 1933)', in S. Durlauf and L. Blume (eds), *The New Palgrave Dictionary of Economics*. Palgrave Macmillan.

Arrow, K.J. 1950. 'A Difficulty in the Concept of Social Welfare', *The Journal of Political Economy*, 58(4): 328–46.

Bellante, D. 2011. 'Edward Chamberlin: Monopolistic Competition and Pareto Optimality', *Journal of Business & Economics Research*, 2(4): 17–26.

Bhagwati, J. 1958. 'Immiserizing Growth: A Geometrical Note', *Review of Economic Studies*, 25(3): 201–5.

———. 1964. 'The Pure Theory of International Trade: A Survey', *The Economic Journal*, 74: 1–84.

———. 1982. 'Directly Unproductive, Profit-seeking (DUP) Activities', *Journal of Political Economy*, 90(5): 988–1002.

———. 1982. 'Lobbying, DUP Activities and Welfare', *Journal of Public Economics*, 19(3): 395–401.

———. 1993. *India in Transition: Freeing the Economy*. Oxford: Clarendon Press.

———. 2004. *In Defense of Globalization*. New Delhi: Oxford University Press.

———. 2008. *Termites in the Trading System*. New York: Oxford University Press.

Bhagwati, J. and B. Hansen. 1973. 'A Theoretical Analysis of Smuggling', *The Quarterly Journal of Economics*, 87(2): 172–87.

Bhagwati, J. and T.N. Srinivasan. 1973. 'The General Equilibrium Theory of Effective Protection and Resource Allocation', *Journal of International Economics*, 3(3): 259–81.

Bharat-Ram, V. 1982. *Towards a Theory of Import Substitution, Exchange Rates and Economic Development*. New Delhi: Oxford University Press.

————. 1997. *The Theory of the Global Firm*. New Delhi: Oxford University Press.

Böhm-Bawerk, E. 1891 [1889]. *The Positive Theory of Capital*, translated from German by W.A. Smart. London: Macmillan.

————. 1898 [1896]. *Karl Marx and the Close of His System: A Criticism*, translated from German by A.M. Macdonald. London: T.F. Unwin.

Chamberlin, E. 1933. *The Theory of Monopolistic Competition*. Boston: Harvard University Press.

Cobb, C. and P. Douglas. 1928. 'A Theory of Production', *American Economic Review*, 18(1): 139–65.

Cusumano, M.A. 1989. *The Japanese Automobile Industry*. Chicago: Harvard University Press.

Desai, M. 2002. *Marx's Revenge: The Resurgence of Capitalism and the Death of Statist Socialism*. London: Verso Books.

————. 2015. *Hubris: Why Economists Failed to Predict the Crisis and How to Avoid the Next One*. London: Yale University Press.

Dow, A. 1773. *History of Hindostan*. London: John Murray.

Engels, F. 1887 [1845]. *The Conditions of the Working Class in England*, translated from German by F. Kelley Wischnewetzky. Leipzig: Otto Wigand.

Fisher, I. 2006a [1912]. *The Purchasing Power of Money: Its Determination and Relation to Credit Interest and Crises*. New York: Macmillan.

————. 2006b [1892]. *Mathematical Investigations in the Theory of Value and Prices, and Appreciation and Interest*. New York: Cosimo.

Ford, M. 2015. *Rise of the Robots*. London: Oneworld Publications.

Friedman, M. and A.J. Schwartz. 2008 [1963]. *A Monetary History of the United States, 1867–1960*. Princeton: Princeton University Press.

Galbraith, J.K. 1958. *The Affluent Society*. Boston: Houghton Mifflin Harcourt.

—————. 1967. *The New Industrial State*. Boston: Houghton Mifflin Harcourt.

—————. 1977. *The Age of Uncertainty*. Boston: Houghton Mifflin Harcourt.

—————. 2001. *The Essential Galbraith*. Boston: Houghton Mifflin Harcourt.

—————. 2009. *The Great Crash 1929*. Boston: Houghton Mifflin Harcourt.

Greenwald, B.C., M. Kohn, and J.E. Stiglitz. 1990. 'Financial Market Imperfections and Productivity Growth', *Journal of Economic Behavior & Organization*, 13(3): 321–45.

Grossman, S.J. and J.E. Stiglitz. 1976. 'Information and Competitive Price Systems', *The American Economic Review*, 66: 246–53.

Gupta, S. 2014. 'National Interest', *India Today*. July 21.

Hansen, A. 1953. *A Guide to Keynes*. New York: McGraw-Hill.

Hayek, F.A. 1934. 'On the Relationship between Investment and Output', *The Economic Journal*, 44(174): 207–31.

—————. 1941. *The Pure Theory of Capital*. Chicago: University of Chicago Press.

—————. 1944. *The Road to Serfdom*. Chicago: University of Chicago Press.

—————. 1978 [1960]. *The Constitution of Liberty*. Chicago: University of Chicago Press.

—————. 1976. *Choice in Currency: A Way to Stop Inflation*, Vol. 48. Auburn: Ludwig von Mises Institute.

—————. 2008. 'Prices and Production', in Joseph T. Salerno (ed.), *Prices and Production and Other Works: F.A. Hayek on Money, the Business Cycle, and the Gold Standard*. Auburn: Ludwig von Mises Institute, pp. 189–330.

Heilbroner, R.L. 1980. *Marxism: For and Against*. New York: W.W. Norton & Company.

—————. 2011. *The Worldly Philosophers: The Lives, Times and Ideas of the Great Economic Thinkers*. New York: Simon and Schuster.

Kahn, R.F. 1931. 'The Relation of Home Investment to Unemployment', *The Economic Journal*, 41(162): 173–98.

Kanth, R.K. (ed.). 1994. *Paradigms in Economic Development: Classic Perspectives, Critiques, and Reflections*. Armonk: M.E. Sharpe.

Keynes, J.M. 1919. *The Economic Consequences of the Peace*. London: Macmillan.

———. 1923. *A Tract on Monetary Reform*. London: Macmillan.

———. 1925. *The Economic Consequences of Mr. Churchill*. New York: Harcourt-Brace.

———. 1936. *General Theory of Employment, Interest and Money*. London: Macmillan.

Kojima, K. 1978. *Japanese Foreign Direct Investment*. Tokyo: Charles E. Tuttle.

Kruger, A. 1974. 'The Political Economy of the Rent-Seeking Society', *American Economic Review*, 64: 291–303.

Lewis, A. 1954. 'Economic Development with Unlimited Supplies of Labour', *The Manchester School*, 22(2): 139–91.

———. 1955. *The Theory of Economic Growth*. Cambridge: Cambridge University Press.

Leontief, W. 1953. 'Domestic Production and Foreign Trade: The American Capital Position Re-examined', *Proceedings of American Psychological Society*, 97(94): 332–49.

———. 1954. 'Mathematics in Economics', *Bulletin of the American Mathematical Society*, 60(3): 215–33.

Lucas, R.E. and T.J. Sargent (eds). 1981. *Rational Expectations and Econometric Practice*. Minneapolis: University of Minnesota Press.

Marshall, A. (ed.). 1952 [1920]. *Principles of Economics*. London: Macmillan.

Marx, K. and F. Engels. 1946 [1848]. *The Communist Manifesto*, translated by A.J.P. Taylor. London: Penguin.

Marx, K. 1990 [1867]. *Capital*, Vol. 1. London: Penguin.

Medema, S.G. and M.C. Antony (eds). 2014. *Paul Samuelson on the History of Economic Analysis*. New York: Cambridge University Press.

Menger, C. 1890. *Principles of Economics*. Auburn: Ludwig von Mises Institute.

Mill, J.S. 2006 [1848]. *Principles of Political Economy*. New York: Cosimo.

Mises, L.V. 1912. *The Theory of Money and Credit*. München and Leipzig: Duncker and Humblot.

Moggridge, D.E. 1992. *Maynard Keynes: An Economist's Biography*. London: Routledge.

BIBLIOGRAPHY

Nasar, S. 2011. *Grand Pursuit: The Story of Economic Genius*. New York: Simon and Schuster.

Nurkse, R. 1959. 'Notes on Unbalanced Growth', *Oxford Economic Papers* (N.S.), 11(3): 295–7.

Ohlin, B. 1933. *Interregional and International Trade*. Cambridge: Harvard University Press.

Padover, S.K. 1978. *Karl Marx: An Intimate Biography*. New York: McGraw-Hill.

Parthasarathi, P. 2011. *Why Europe Grew Rich and Asia Did Not: Global Economic Divergence, 1600–1850*. Cambridge: Cambridge University Press.

Piketty, T. 2014. *Capital in the Twenty-First Century*. Cambridge: Harvard University Press.

Phillips, A.W. 1958. 'The Relation between Unemployment and the Rate of Change of Money Wage Rates in the United Kingdom, 1861–1957', *Economica*, 25(100): 283–99.

Rajan, R.R. 2010. *Fault Lines: How Hidden Fractures Still Threaten the World Economy*. Princeton: Princeton University Press.

Ricardo, D. 1973 [1817]. *The Principles of Political Economy and Taxation*. London: John Murray.

Robins, N. 2006. *The Corporation that Changed the World: How the East India Company Shaped the Modern Multinational*. Hyderabad: Orient Longman.

Robinson, J. 1954. *The Economics of Imperfect Competition*. New York: Macmillan.

Rothschild, E. 2001. *Economic Sentiments: Adam Smith, Condorcet, and the Enlightenment*. Cambridge: Harvard University Press.

Rowntree, B. 1901. *Poverty: A Study in Town Life*. London: Macmillian.

Samuelson, P.A. 1983 [1947]. *Foundations of Economic Analysis*. Cambridge: Harvard University Press.

————. 1967. 'On the History of Economic Analysis: Selected Essays', *Quarterly Journal of Economics*, 8: 592–609.

Samuelson, P.A. and W.D. Nordhaus. 1992 [1948]. *Economics: An Introductory Analysis*, fourteenth edition. New York: McGraw-Hill.

Say, J.B. 1821. *A Treatise on Political Economy; or the Production, Distribution and Consumption of Wealth*. Boston: Wells and Lilly.

Schumpeter, J.A. 1912 [1934]. *The Theory of Economic Development*. Cambridge: Harvard University Press.

————. 1939. *Business Cycles: A Theoretical, Historical and Statistical Analysis of the Capitalist Process*. New York: McGraw-Hill.

————. 1942. *Capitalism, Socialism and Democracy*. London: Allen and Unwin.

Schwarzschild, L. 1947. *The Red Prussian: The Life and Legend of Karl Marx*. New York: Charles Scribner's Sons.

Sen, A. 1960. *The Choice of Techniques*. Oxford: Basil Blackwell.

————. 1970. 'The Impossibility of the Paretian Liberal', *Journal of Political Economy*, 78(1): 152–7.

————. 1981. *Poverty and Famines: An Essay of Entitlement and Deprivation*. Oxford: Clarendon Press.

————. 1976. 'Poverty: An Ordinal Approach to Measurement', *Econometrica: Journal of the Econometric Society*, 44(2): 219–31.

————. 1984 [1970]. *Collective Choice and Social Welfare*. New York: North Holland.

————. 1999. *Development as Freedom*. New York: Knopf.

————. 2009. 'Capitalism Beyond the Crisis', *The New York Review of Books*, 56(5): 26.

————. 2011. *The Idea of Justice*. Cambridge: Harvard University Press.

Sharma, R. 2016. *The Rise and Fall of Nations*. London: Penguin-Random House.

Skidelsky, R. 2010. *Keynes: The Return of the Master*. New York: Public Affairs.

Skousen, M. 2001. *The Making of Modern Economics: The Lives and Ideas of Great Thinkers*. New York: M.E. Sharpe.

————. 2007. *The Big Three in Economics: Adam Smith, Karl Marx, and John Maynard Keynes*. New York: M.E. Sharpe.

Smith, A. 2009 [1759]. *The Theory of Moral Sentiments*. London: Penguin.

————. 1776. *The Wealth of Nations*. Chicago: University of Chicago Press.

Spiegel, H.W. 1971. *The Growth of Economic Thought*. Durham: Duke University Press.

Stiglitz, J.E. 1993. *World Bank Policy Research Report*, no. 12351, vol. 1. New York: Oxford University Press.

————. 1979. 'Equilibrium in Product Markets with Imperfect Information', *American Economic Review*, 69(2): 339–45.

Stiglitz, J.E. and A. Weiss. 1992. 'Asymmetric Information in Credit Markets and Its Implications for Macro-economics', *Oxford Economic Papers*, 44(4): 694–724.

Urata, Shujiro. 1998. 'The Development of the Motor Vehicle Industry in Post-Second World War Japan', *Industry and Development*, 24.

Walras, L. 1954 [1874]. *Elements of Pure Economics*. London: George Allen and Unwin.

Wapshott, N. 2011. 'Keynes-Hayek: The Clash that Defined Modern Economics', *The Quarterly Journal of Austrian Economics*, 14(4): 474–9.

Wicksell, K. 1936. *Interest and Prices: A Study of the Causes Regulating the Value of Money*. London: Macmillan.

Witt, U. 2002. 'How Evolutionary Is Schumpeter's Theory of Economic Development?', *Industry and Innovation*, 9(1–2): 7–22.

Yamazawa, I. 1986. 'Full Utilisation of Foreign Trade and Industrialisation: East Asian Experiences', paper presented at the sixth International Economic Association, World Congress. New Delhi.

About the Author

Vinay Bharat-Ram hails from the pioneering industrial family of Lala Shri Ram and is the chairman of DCM Limited, a company with interests in engineering, information technology, real estate, and textiles.

Bharat-Ram has three strands to his career. Business, of course, is one of them, but equally important are his other two interests—academics and music. In his earlier years, he taught at the Indian Institute of Management Ahmedabad and the Faculty of Management Studies, University of Delhi. Presently, he is honorary visiting professor of economics at the management department of the Indian Institute of Technology Delhi, where he has been teaching for the last thirty years.

As a musician, he is a well-known classical vocalist and has performed all over India and abroad. His recordings spanning forty years are available on Red Ribbon (http://www.redribbon.in/).

Among the honours he has received are the National Citizens Award (1990) for entrepreneurship from the prime minister of India and the National Excellence Award for Art and Culture (1996-7) from the T.P. Jhunjhunwala Foundation.

His publications include *From the Brink of Bankruptcy* (2011), *The Theory of the Global Firm* (1997), and *Towards a Theory of Import Substitution Exchange Rates and Economic Development* (1982).

During the period when he was writing and researching for this book, his dog—Professor Orio—who is his constant companion, sniffed every new document or book and then relapsed next to his feet in deep contemplation!